MW01193729

BE YOUR BRAND

Regan Hillyer

© Copyright 2015, Regan Hillyer International
All rights reserved.

ISBN 978-0-473-35590-6
Title Be Your Brand: From Unknown To Unforgettable In 60 Days
Author Regan Hillyer
Format Softcover
Publication Date 04/2016

This book or any portion thereof may not be reproduced or used in any manner whatsoever without the express written permission of the publisher except for the use of brief quotations in a book review.

Created in Bali, Indonesia and brought to you, wherever you are in the world.

Receive Regan's FREE bestselling book: *Make Your Passion Into Your Paycheck* **when you subscribe to http://www.reganhillyer.com/**

Get in touch with Regan Hillyer:
Website: www.reganhillyer.com
Email: info@reganhillyer.com
Facebook: https://www.facebook.com/ReganHillyer
Twitter: https://twitter.com/ReganHillyer
Instagram: http://instagram.com/reganhillyer/
LinkedIn: https://www.linkedin.com/in/reganhillyer
YouTube: http://ht.ly/WxZLc

ABOUT THE AUTHOR

*R*egan is a "serial entrepreneur", coach and an educator. Regan has founded several companies, invested in real estate and has transformed the lives of thousands across many different industries.

For over a decade, Regan has been obsessed with what makes people successful. Her mission is to help you unlock your true potential, become wildly successful, and make an impact in this world.

Regan's expertise falls in several different areas, including training, empowerment, music, real estate, mindset, and education. She feels extraordinarily fortunate to have the freedom and excitement that she experiences in every area of her life. It's authentic, extensive, and complete. She feels strongly that everyone deserves to have what she experiences day-to-day.

However, it wasn't all fun and roses in the beginning for Regan. She tried to do everything right. She went to a great school, worked really hard, got good grades, yet she never truly felt that she was doing what she was put on this planet to do.

After moving alone to the UK following an unsuccessful attempt to figure out her life's goal, Regan completed a degree in Architecture, only to remain unfulfilled and uncertain about what her future held.

It soon became apparent to Regan that there was a deep longing inside her to create success for herself in all areas of her life and lead others so that they are able to do this as well. This spurred a large amount of personal development and training, engaging in some of the world's top mindset and wealth coaches to shift Regan from where she was, to where she wanted to be.

Regan now runs international programs, helping thousands of

people reach their true performance potential. Heading up a motivated, hungry, and passionate team spanning from Bali to Auckland, Victoria, New South Wales, The Cook Islands, California, Florida, and Arizona, who are fueled by success and are extremely passionate about their tribe, their vibe, and getting extraordinary results daily.

Powered by a vision where every human has the ability to unlock their greatness and achieve extensive financial and personal abundance, their mission is to disrupt the world's version of "normal", and help people to become wildly successful, right now.

If you want to get in touch, sign up for their free newsletter (to get first access on any new creations), or if you are interested in hearing more about The Be Your Brand LIVE Masterminds (in-person and online) then simply go to: www.reganhillyer.com - they'd love to hear from you.

Plus, their tribe has the coolest, most passionate, edgy vibe — we know you'd fit right in here.

Receive Regan's FREE bestselling book: *Make Your Passion Into Your Paycheck* **when you subscribe to http://www.reganhillyer.com/**

PREFACE

As I sit here writing this in Bali, Indonesia, it really all feels like a blur. Sixty days ago I was in a place where I was confused, overwhelmed and seriously lacking focus when it came to my personal brand. The biggest reason was, simply, because I didn't have a personal brand!

I was the person who could have gone in twenty different directions. Should I be this? Should I create this? Should I launch this? What if it doesn't work? The questions were endless.

Fast forward sixty days and I sit here with a well-established brand that is already in profit, clearly defined by physical results.

And I'm here to tell you that you can do this, too.

Amongst the confusion and the questions and the lack of clarity, there's one thing I know for sure — you ABSOLUTELY have a personal brand that just hasn't been established yet.

You are an incredible, unique, amazing individual, unlike any other person walking the planet right now. You have a message, a voice, and a soul. Yet here's the challenge right now. You're not branded. Or, you're not branded well.

Because here's what's interesting: sixty days ago, I was the same "me" as I am right now. I was still Regan. I had the same values, the same beliefs, the same mission and the same voice. I just wasn't positioning myself right, or, at all. I wasn't stepping 100% into my greatness, simply because I didn't know HOW.

Now, if you're someone who is a little afraid (or hugely afraid!) to step 100% into your greatness, that's normal and you need to get to work on YOU and your mindset, but that's not what this book is about. This book is designed to give you the strategy. The step-by-step system as to how I went from being globally unknown to now being unforgettable, in just sixty days.

We're talking being in thousands of dollars of profit, connecting with key people of influence, being picked up by huge media outlets internationally, speaking on international stages, tripling social media presence, having a much bigger impact than ever before and playing a much, MUCH bigger game.

The question is, are YOU ready to "Be Your Brand"?

Sit back, relax, enjoy the book, then take massive action.

CONTENTS

INTRODUCTION

This book is a step by step guide as to how I built my global empire from scratch.

It is broken into three simple sections:

- Developing Your Brand
- Launching Your Brand
- Accelerating Your Brand

Here's what I know for SURE!

You ALREADY have a brand, you may just not be "branded" yet.

Or, you may own a company, but quite possibly you do not have a personal brand.

How do I know you have a brand?

Simple.

You have a heart beat.

You have a deep message that you are called to share with this world.

You are destined for greatness.

And last time I checked, there is only one version of you, so when you do develop and launch your brand, it will be entirely unique, entirely, well, YOU!

It's just a matter of unlocking "that" and making a choice to make a massive impact in this world...

My mission is to unlock your greatness, disrupt your version of "normal" and let you know that you can become wildly successful, now. A world traveler at heart, I pride myself on making a massive impact in this world and showing people that they can be extraordinary, because there's lots of room at the top!

I am a best selling author, an international speaker, entrepreneur and coach. I have founded The Be Your Brand Mastermind LIVE, The Online Empire Builder, Your SuccessHub Weekly Success Coaching, amongst other incredible live events and online programs. Everything I do gives back and supports the Lumière Project, with the mission to help people ignite their flames and unleash their true message on the world.

I am an expert when it comes to working with people one-on-one, as well as in small mastermind groups, and I would love to help you create a business and a life that you love, allowing you to "have it all" in every area of your life, on your terms!

A Kiwi girl who tried to do it all right — go to school, get good grades, go to university... And one day I figured out that there was definitely more to life. With a ridiculous work ethic, a heart of service and a laptop, I've created my socially conscious empire from scratch. With a global approach to success and development, I'm here to tell you that you really CAN have it all...

I don't do labels, but if I had to have one, it would be a "serial entrepreneur" because, like you, there are many things that I love taking to the next level.

I believe that you need to bring your complete game to the business table and if you want to stand out and be successful in today's world, then that includes your personality, your vibe, your tribe and, most importantly, your hunger to succeed. I'm known to deliver high quality, out of the box, say it like it is, break the rules, business and personal development training.

This step-by-step guide ignores many traditional rules in business. And if you're someone who's in love with the "right" way or the "secret system" then I suggest you stop reading right now, as this book will most likely do nothing other than frustrate you.

However, if you are a rock star, an artist, an individual who KNOWS that you have something powerful to unleash on the world, then this will be right up your alley.

So sit back, relax, and dig right in.

And if at any point you're itching to connect with me, please head on over to www.reganhillyer.com, or connect with me on social media because I am a real human and I love connecting with people who get my vibe.

Now let's get cranking...

PART 1
DEVELOPING YOUR BRAND

This section is all about unlocking your greatness, encouraging you to take massive action and ultimately make an incredible difference in this world.

*H*old your horses.
I know you're excited.
I know you want to dive straight into this.
I know you're ready to unleash your true message on the world.
But let's get real, we have some work to do first!

We need to firstly get very clear on what you're looking to achieve, what your true message to the world actually is and begin to form a realistic, doable plan before we launch you into the big bad world!

Here's the first thing you need to know:

Brands are an asset. They should be created, developed, and managed with great care and due diligence. Having an overall process to create a successful strategy for a brand is essential to achieving long-term positive performance. Finding out who you are in the most authentic way is the groundwork for creating and building genuine personal brands. The process for building personal brands is a science, combined with a lot of artistic license.

Now here's the thing. When it comes to personal branding, YOU are your brand. So ultimately, your brand should just be an extension of yourself. You, sharing your thoughts, beliefs, talents, fears, failures and successes with the world.

Let's examine what it means to think like a brand. Genuine brands clearly follow a strategy so that they will be perceived as distinctive from other choices, more relevant to their customers, consumers, associates, and influencers; and they offer superior perceived value.

GETTING CLEAR ON WHAT A BRAND IS

To be sure we are on the same page, let's be clear on what exactly a brand is. A brand is emotions, reputations, sounds, your name, a design, or anything that separates you from everyone else. For example, the golden arches of McDonald's became the brand symbol and separated this product from any other restaurant of fast food. Even kids recognize the golden arches, unfortunately! (But don't get me started on a huge chat about health and what we should be feeding our children!)

It is common to brand on the level of business. However, on a personal level, branding is becoming just as important. After all, businesses are merely people working with people and that is what makes it a valuable relationship. It is from this point of view that your personal brand should be created.

There are professional opportunities where building a personal brand is now extremely important and powerful. These opportunities can include industry recognition, better contacts for your company and your tribe, and a greater ability to stand out from the rest. If you are looking for some improvement in your career for example, your ideal company and possible bosses should relate your personal brand with something necessary for that particular company and team. If what you are looking for is to grow company sales, you will want your work clients to relate your personal brand with the feeling of long term success, trust and satisfaction.

Doing what you love and following your passion leads many people into becoming entrepreneurs and branching out of their career at one point or another. For many professionals, the ultimate career goal is being self-employed. Naturally, there are tons of benefits as well as risks that come with becoming your own brand. Here are a few expectations of what will most likely occur.

When you work for other people, you help them in building their own vision and brand. Now that you decided to step out and do your own thing, you get complete control — one hundred percent of everything, including every brand detail involved. This includes who you want your audience or your tribe to be and what message you would like to send out. This is a dream come true for those who have been thinking about developing their own brand for some time now. All of you artists, creators and passionate rock stars, I know you're understanding this right now!

Making all the decisions is one reason many people decide to go off on their own and become a brand. Not only will you be the boss, you will be responsible for everything from start to finish. Of course, at this point you will also be accountable for all the mistakes that could happen, but the same goes for all the successes. After a while, you will soon develop discernment about what a good deal looks like and also develop tons of self discipline in the process. On the whole, you become a better, more developed person overall.

Another reason many individuals leave their supervised, traditional jobs to become their own brand is to do what they truly love, one hundred percent of the time. They want to commit to doing what they love without any interruptions. One of the benefits of doing this is being flexible enough for setting your own schedule and devoting the necessary time you feel is needed to focusing on your dreams and accomplishing your goals.

Of course there is uncertainty when the next check will come for you in the mail. This is the main difference between being employed and being self-employed. All you had to do when you were employed was to wait in the mail for your check to arrive. Now that you stepped out of your comfort zone, it is time to create your own paycheck, as you are responsible for all the money your company makes.

Being your own brand involves a promise and a commitment or pledge made to assure the recipient, that he or she can trust that certain expectations will be fulfilled. It goes beyond a simple statement of intent to a higher ethical level that puts at risk the grantor's honor and integrity if the commitment goes unfulfilled.

The consistent fulfillment of purpose is the essence of the Oprah brand, for instance. The reason for viewer loyalty is the emotional connection to the brand, as well as the foundation for Oprah's success. For those of us responsible for fulfilling our commitment, it is our common purpose that is widely shared at all levels of the company. It gives us direction, inspires us, and unleashes our passion and commitment to convert our intentions into great results. As consumers, we are constantly promised that we will be inspired by the food and beverages we consume, the products and services we buy, and the organizations that serve us. The organizations that actually fulfill these commitments gain our trust, our loyalty, and our business. In our other roles as a brand, we want to be inspired by a purpose, the work we do, and the integrity with which we do it. We want to be part of responsible organizations that meet or the commitments they make so that we have reason to be proud of where we work. Promises made and fulfilled are the foundation, not only for consumer loyalty, but also the passion, commitment, and loyalty required to create and maintain successful organizations. This book provides the insights strategies, and mechanisms for people who sincerely desire to make meaningful brands of themselves that inspire the loyalty of their customers and fellow associates. This philosophy is perfect for individuals and organizations that want to build genuine brands or relationships that are trusted and admired. It requires a sincere and real commitment to customers', associates and shareholders' well-being and satisfaction.

Making a real promise means caring about others in a way that is heartfelt, and not just a great business proposition. Imagine a world where everyone makes a promise and keeps it. I am here to provide a practical understanding of why the promise philosophy is so important to him or her and how anyone can use it to enhance the lives of customers.

The search for substance in competitive strategic thinking has moved from advertising to marketing to branding, and more recently to promise. Many leading businesses and intellectual thought leaders are beginning to talk about the importance of a commitment to a promise in all types of organizations. My philosophy separates substance from hype and provides a practical guide for any organization or individual on how to make the right promise and how to keep real promises to customers, associates, and shareholders alike.

The concepts I created revolve around the importance of focusing on how a brand wants its tribe, associates, influencers, and, for that matter, all of its stakeholders to feel. It is this paradigm shift that provides the kind of success that truly admired brands enjoy.

To become a one-of-a-kind brand, an individual must think like a "genuine brand," and this requires a different mindset, perspective, and strategy from the usual. Successful individual brands need to be perceived as having a distinctive commitment to their customers and consumers that delivers emotional and functional benefits. When an individual thinks and acts like a "real brand", the entire organization understands what the promise is all about and how to deliver the right experience. Everyone from the CEO to the frontline associate has the same mindset.

Successful implementation of a promise initiative requires that everyone in the organization be on board. It's not optional. Leading brands that deliver on their promise will benefit from enhanced customer satisfaction and profitable pricing opportunities, as well as increased pride and the power of a positive experience. The key to becoming a successful genuine brand is to focus on providing distinctive and relevant experiences for customers that provide lasting and memorable positive impressions. Genuine brands make a promise, and they deliver on that promise consistently, eagerly, and at their customer's convenience. The power of a promise is based on what customers say about a brand to their friends and their feelings toward the brand. In a word association exercise, when consumers are asked, "What is a brand?" the most frequent response is: A name. Consumers see brand names every day; they are bombarded with thousands of brand impressions in print and across all forms of electronic media. It's impossible to escape them.

Don't get me wrong. Having a good brand name is important and offers several advantages. However, there is much more to a strategy for a brand than a name. Successful brands lead the way. They become their promise, and they behave like a guarantee. Yet brands really exist only in people's minds. Brands tell customers whether something will make them feel better or make their life easier, better, solve a problem, or fulfill a need or desire. *The Random House Dictionary of the English Language* defines a brand as: "A kind or variety of something distinguished by some distinctive characteristic." It is the distinctive traits that separate brands from commodity items in consumers' minds.

1. Is it truly distinctive or different in a manner that is important and valued by its customers?
2. Is it committed to providing certain emotional and functional benefits for its customers?
3. Does it consistently fulfill its promise and deliver on its commitments? Genuine brands exist only to add value. They understand that people make real-life decisions every day on both an emotional and a functional level. Genuine brands make promises that make you feel great about your experience. Then they deliver on that promise. Genuine brands treat people right and exceed expectations.

REASONS FOR CREATING YOUR OWN BRAND

In building and creating your own brand, you may want to do this for the purpose of:

- Laying the foundations of your success in the future, no matter what your definition of success is
- Build communities online to further increase opportunities in your profession
- Grow your network professionally so you open more opportunities
- Land better company clients to create more efficiency for your company
- Win more company clients to increase your earnings and your sales
- Create a bigger impact in this world and also create a bigger amount of money in the process

WHO ARE YOU?

Before you develop a personal brand and launch it out to the world, it is important to be yourself, authentically. Remember — as I touched on earlier, you actually already have a brand, except it has not been established just yet. You no longer need to hide or search to hide, as you ARE the brand. Realizing your potential sooner rather than later is going to go a long way towards helping you establish a truly authentic brand.

Start by asking yourself these questions:

- Who are you?
- What do you believe about the world?
- If you were to know, what is your true message that you need the world to hear?
- What frustrates you?
- What excites you?

And this is just the beginning…

The clearer you can get on who YOU actually are, the more powerful, authentic and impactful your brand will be.

GETTING CLEAR ON YOUR VISION

Let's chat on vision. Vision is the bigger picture, it's what is driving you every day. Ultimately your vision should be so powerful that you are willing to die for it. And I don't say that lightly. It is the essence of your brand, and ultimately in personal branding, the essence of YOU as a unique individual.

When it comes to personal branding, your vision often develops into a promise that is intended to characterize how you want your tribe to feel and what you want them to also be empowered by.

The promise should become the heart and soul of your brand and set the tone for everything your brand does. It's the internal battle cry that is intended to set a brand's expectations for every team member, agent, or representative. It dictates how the brand wants its tribe to feel about their experience.

The way you want to unfold is a direction only you can determine. It is not easy to control every life aspect. However, you can develop steps for achieving this and create long term vision as well. The vision of your life needs to make an inclusion of how you see yourself in ten, twenty or even fifty years. Consider your life elements and what makes you smile — a challenging corporate job, a beach house, a family? There are really no wrong or right answers — only the ones that apply to you. Just like everything else, there are a few things you need to do to create your own brand.

Basically, what separates you from the rest of the globe is your personal brand. To start creating your own brand you will need to create your own vision for your brand. Do this by organizing your thoughts. Basically, you will want others to perceive you this way and this is also the way you want to live your personal and professional life.

To create your vision, it is necessary to really understand the needs of your tribe. If you really want to understand your tribe's needs, you must walk in their shoes. Ask yourself, how will your brand really enhance your tribe's lives? What drives you?

Why does this drive you?

What exactly do you want to achieve?

What is the message you want the world to hear, now?

When developing your vision, I suggest that you sit down and write out a list of fifty plus words that you would use to describe your brand

and where it is headed. From here, the strongest themes driving your brand will start to become apparent. Like every exercise in this book, make sure your vision is true to your authentic self and so strong that it really is the essence of YOU and who you are.

AUTHENTICITY

Personal branding rests on the foundation of authenticity. This is the ability of tapping into your individual, humble, genuine, human quality from which your character, personality and identity stem from.

If you are not showing up through your brand in a way that is completely, one hundred percent authentic to you then trust me, it is going to end in disaster: Be it financial disaster, or simply just resulting in you feeling totally unsatisfied or unfulfilled.

So let's start with the end in mind and make sure that every step in developing your brand, every step of the way, is completely aligned with you, your core message and what you want to shake the world with.

Otherwise, you may as well quit right now…

Your authentic self appearing constantly through your brand creates a "genuine brand". For instance, when an organization thinks and acts like a "genuine brand", the entire organization understands what the promise is all about and how to deliver the right experience. Everyone from the CEO to the frontline associate has the same mindset. Successful implementation of a promise initiative requires that everyone in the organization be on board. It's not optional! Leading brands that deliver on their promise will benefit from enhanced customer satisfaction and profitable pricing opportunities, as well as increased pride and the power of a positive experience. The power of a promise is based on what customers say about a brand to their friends and their feelings toward the brand. In a word association exercise, when consumers are asked, "What is a brand?" the most frequent response is: We see brand names every day; they are with thousands of brand impressions in print and across all forms of electronic media. It's impossible to escape them. Don't get me wrong. Having a good brand name is important and offers several advantages. However, there is much more to a strategy for a brand than a name. Successful brands lead the way. They become their promise, and they behave like a guarantee. Yet brands really exist only in people's minds. Brands tell customers whether something will make them feel better or make their life easier, better, solve a problem, or fulfill a need or desire.

DISCOVERING YOUR DRIVING VALUES

Your values are one of the most important things that you need to get clear on when developing your brand. Your values are what drive your life, your decisions and ultimately your results. They are at your being's core and when making decisions, your values automatically click into action. Everyone makes mistakes once in a while and maybe you don't refer to your values. However, when you make life decisions it is your values that you usually consider.

The following set of values may be what you have:

- Freedom
- Ambition
- Community
- Friends
- Family

To people, values define the stuff that is considered most important. When you need to make a decision such as whether or not you are going to take on a new career, it is with your personal values that you consult. Ask yourself what the best decision would be in terms of values on the list such as friends and family.

On your list, there is no limit of values you can add. They are yours alone. Consider your life situations, feelings and people that make you happy the most. This is usually where your values are found.

The goal of personal brand building is not just to grow your company or achieve further success, it is about ultimately finding happiness. When you really consider that personal brands are simply an extension of you and who you are, then ultimately the decisions you make within your brand will result in more happiness if these are aligned with your values. Many individuals know other people who are successful in their work but are not happy. This is due to the fact that it was only later on that they realized how much they valued their family and vice versa, those who may have a great family life only later realize that they lack fulfillment due to the challenges of their profession. You will know how to approach your personal vision for your brand if you make understanding your values your priority.

It is a good idea to hire a team with similar values to your brand. People that have almost the same values as the brand that is hiring will be likely to meet the needs of the brand more, and tend to adapt to new roles much faster. They also tend to fall in love with the brand's vision very easily and often will want to be a part of the team for a very long time.

Go through the things that make you happy in life. Realize that there is no equality when it comes to values. List values according to priority and how important they are to you.

You may be faced with decisions in life and situations that are at odds with your values. For instance, when considering new work, it may fit into your intelligence and ambition values, but will require more time away from your job and family if they do not have the same values that you believe in.

WHAT IS YOUR PASSION?

The whole point of developing your personal brand is so that you can do what you love, every single day and of course, create an empire and a legacy from doing just that.

Which brings us to the question:

What do you like doing with your time?

Whatever the answer, these are your passions. Generally, passions are different from values although they do overlap at times. For instance, your highest values might be family life and your passions might be playing with your kids or going out to dinner with your spouse. There is an intersection of passions and values but these are also different. Identifying your passion in order for you to know what is most rewarding to you in life will go a long way towards creating your personal brand. Identifying your passion is the key to creating a personal brand successfully. Make it your objective to experience your passion in your life professionally.

Passions are things that keep you interested. Passions make you want to investigate and intrigue you. For personal driven reasons, they make you want to get better. Passions are things you would do that you would pay for or would do even without getting paid for it.

A passion can be both professional and personal. Identify your professional and personal passions. This will give you a clue about what drives your life professionally. When you are not working, you are usually doing something you are passionate about.

Professional passions might include technology, smart phones and design. Personal passions might include the outdoors, travel and family.

Aside from the values of a person, these passions provide a clear vision for where you want to be in two, five or twenty years. The moment you identify what you are passionate about, it starts becoming clear what profession type you are best matched for and what would bring you satisfaction.

Identifying your traits will help you further unlock what you are passionate about and ultimately create your personal brand. These are aspects unique to your own personality that help in shaping you as a person. Things like traits are what give others a key within your mind. Some examples of personality traits include:

- Neuroticism
- Agreeableness
- Extraversion
- Conscientiousness
- Openness to experience

Each trait mentioned above is scaled and assessed. Every person tends to be somewhere on various scales making up their character. When it comes to traits, there really are no right and wrong answers. What you are doing is simply making an identification of where you stand and how you want your personal brand to unfold. It is good to know where you stand right now. Also, know that you can always change. This way you can make plans for change if you feel like a change is necessary.

With your peers, friends and family, discuss who you are. These people will help you get an idea of who you are as a person and it is going to be good to listen to them. Ask people how they perceive you. Inquire about what they believe you value, what they feel your traits are as well as your passions. The exterior perception might not be the same as your own self-perceptions or they may indeed be aligned.

No matter what the verdict is, the information you get from asking other people about you will help you understand things better and where you want to be in your personal and professional life. In the end, you will live a life that is more fulfilling if you build your personal brand. Get feedback from peers, friends and family to know how aligned your goals are with your personal brand.

THE POWER OF YOUR UNIQUE STORY

In personal branding, your story is everything! I always hear people tossing their story to the side and saying that it's not important, when it is really one of THE most important parts of your brand. Why? Because it allows people to connect with you and your brand on a deeper level and allows people to learn through your life experiences at the same time.

People that do realise the power in their story often simply focus on their successes, their wins, the great things that have happened in their life, and although those are important, what is potentially MORE important is unlocking your unique failures and the critical turning points in time where others can learn and ultimately fast track their success.

DISCOVERING YOUR UNIQUE FAILURES

Often what we perceive to be our most terrible, unsuccessful, awful moments of failure, eventually become our biggest glories. There is power in your failures and also money locked away in your failures. I always say, "The bigger the failure, the easier it is to have a big impact and create a lot of money." Why? There will always be people willing to invest in you to learn from your experiences so they can short-cut their road to success, by-pass the failures and achieve what they want faster.

Dig deep into what you believe your "failures" are in your life. These could be big things, for example being broke or homeless, or, things which people often deem to be not as big (but actually are) such as being totally lost, confused or unfilled. Any times that are not spent ecstatically happy and moving forward, can be dived into deeper because there are absolutely lessons in there!!

Unlocking Your Critical Turning Points in Time

Your unique, critical turning points in time are potentially even more powerful than your unique failures. Your critical turning points are that slight moment in time, where during or directly after your perceived failure at the time, you make a decision or something happens which creates change, often in an upwards or positive direction. Those "aha" moments are absolutely critical when it comes to sharing your compelling story and also helping others unlock how you have achieved what you have achieved. So dive deep on this and make sure with every failure that you list when defining your story, to work out the critical turning point in time that shortly followed it.

WHAT MAKES YOU STAND OUT?

When you are developing a brand, think about what makes you stand out. What do people remember? Human memory has found that the mind remembers things that are unique and distinctive. The goal is to be perceived as a unique product and not be just one of many in a sea of the same-old, same-old. If you think genuine brands are primarily the reason for marketing departments that burn the midnight oil while advertising messages that push your message across, you wouldn't be wrong. The process of advertising involves literally broadcasting thousands of bits of information throughout the course of a day, including advertising online and through message boards. The ones that are authentic tend to stick in the mind and truly affect decision making. Once there is a connection made with consumers on a meaningful and emotional level; that is to say, your product genuinely fulfills a need or/and a desired feeling, then this translates to purchases made and income. These are genuine brands that make the money. A genuine brand is defined as: "The internalized impressions received by customers and consumers resulting in a position in their mind's eye based on perceived value."

Perceptions, once formed, are difficult to alter. This is why many of the dot-coms failed. They did not have promise, or if they made one, chances are it was broken. During the height of the initial e-commerce surge, do you know how many e-commerce sites offered free shirts with the promise of delivery in time for Christmas? How many could not deliver on that promise? The vast majority of them never saw the next holiday shopping season. Why? Because they found out too late that once a promise was made, customers expected them not only to keep it but make good on it as well if the promise was broken. Internet companies were not alone in the unfulfilled promise department. Many companies fail to provide personal service when it is needed most. How easy is it to contact a real, live, empowered, decision-making customer service representative on the weekends? It is the experience — the interaction between customers and the company that shapes and drives a brand's perceptions, attitudes, and buying decisions.

This process begins when the promise is made and extends to when the promise is delivered. The brand's ability to live up to its promise determines whether customers, newly acquired or long term, are loyal and return. It also determines how frequently they return. But most importantly, the promise determines how they feel. New York Life's media advertising expresses the promise philosophy well. Its advertising asks the question, "Does a promise come with an expiration date? Is it a month, a year, decades from now? At New York Life we make promises that have no expiration date." The successful implementation of an innovative and distinctive strategy for any organization's brand, regardless of size are tightly linked to its ability to succeed beyond the first few years of operation — and prosper as well. At the end of the day, brands that live up to their promise have the opportunity to enjoy a healthy bottom line.

A successful brand reflects the successful implementation of a strong promise. The benefit is that competitors with emotional links already have strong loyalty among them and do not need to use excessive marketing dollars to generate store traffic. As you can see, when it comes to understanding consumer motivations, the attributes which can differentiate a good brand compared to its competitors' positions on the brand can be very helpful in developing a strong following. A good brand that becomes successful places the customer first. It is a state of mind, the heart and soul of an organization. A promise defines how to feel. It defines the benefits organizations want for their customers, both emotional and functional, that the customers should expect to receive when experiencing a brand's products or service.

THE WOW FACTOR

What's the "wow" about? It is when customers, tribe members, constituents, clients, and the public consider the brand to be a "friend."

Rewarding loyalty can be a wonderful strategy. When it becomes the sole reason for customers returning, it can become something else, something I refer to as "brand bribery." Brand bribery lurks in commodity-driven industries characterized by a discernible lack of differentiated products or outstanding service — THE TRUST FACTOR. We use the word "genuine" because it means authentic, and something that's genuine is supposed to be real and trusted. At the core of a genuine brand is the feeling of trust. The importance of trust cannot be overstated. Organizations that believe in creating genuine brands are able to benefit from brands with integrity.

Brand integrity forms a foundation for trust and interpersonal warmth and loyalty. It builds credibility and leads to a personal reputation. By creating predictability, it enables others to predict your judgments and to act on reliable, accurate information. It all but eliminates the need for associates to wonder and discuss what your agenda is and whether you mean what you say. These immediate consequences of integrity echo far beyond the attitudes and behaviors of associates and directly impact the customer's experience.

CREATING EXCEPTIONAL PERCEIVED BRAND VALUE

Perceived value is at the crux of everyone's perception of their experience with your brand. Often, companies are singularly concerned about price of their products. While price is important, it's only one part of the whole. As a general rule, customers develop their perception of value through a subconscious feeling as a result of comparing the brand's product and service offerings with those of its competitors based on their own needs, preferences, buying behavior, and characteristics. Thus, a customer's perception of value constantly changes to deliver value and delight customers and is deeply rooted in the promise. Genuine brands create delighted customers who believe and trust the brand's ability to deliver value and are willing to pay an amount greater than the total cost of the products and services. Profits serve as one measure of how well a brand is creating delighted customers. However, long-term profit is more important than a strategy that increases profits in the short term at the expense of future brand equity. In some cases, customers may perceive value to mean "low in price." A marketing position of lowest price is the most difficult to sustain and generally is an indication that the brand or organization has become a commodity in the minds of consumers. The only distinctive point of difference that commodities usually have is price. Genuine brands understand that a lowest-price strategy does not necessarily guarantee customer loyalty. Customers looking for the lowest price will primarily be loyal to the price, not the brand. On the other hand, when customers perceive that the brand has established a brand that consistently delivers value, it now has the foundation to become a genuine brand. As a result, genuine brands enjoy higher degrees of profitability, customer loyalty and enhanced brand equity. When an organization is "thinking like a brand," everyone understands that customers are buying more than just products or services. Genuine brands never focus solely on a product alone; they are committed to their brand as a product and service. To refer to a product alone is to say that the customer doesn't care about time convenience, feelings, and overall satisfaction. When creating a brand, the perceived benefit should exceed the ability to deliver the positive perceived value which is determined by consumers' perceptions of brand's benefits versus its total cost, both functional and of course, emotional.

A brand concept of a guarantee is based on a philosophy of signals. Promise signals can include everything from customer feedback to customer service representatives on the phone. The important promise signal is the organization's commitment to how they make the customers feel when they have a service problem. Ace Hardware is a good example of the value of a "no-hassle" guarantee. When I return an item to Ace, I'm never made to feel bad, nor do I get hassled. In fact, Ace makes customers feel just as good when they return as they did about the original purchase. This is a service signal. Ace is actually a cooperative of 4,600 stores owned primarily by individual operators, and the company has recently enjoyed great success. As Ray Griffith, the CEO, says, "We come to work every day on behalf of the entrepreneur. We have a chip on our shoulder about the big boxes, and we like that. We like being the underdog. America loves the underdog." It's clear that Ace wants to distinguish its customer experience from other "big box" stores (national home improvement megastores). It's interesting to note that, in 2007, Ace Hardware ("The Helpful Place") was ranked the highest in customer satisfaction for major home improvement stores by J.D. Power and Associates.

Another great example is Wolferman's. Wolferman's was founded in 1888 and has been a proud purveyor of specialty foods for over 100 years. In 1910, it started making the unique English muffins, which is only one of their premium specialty foods. Wolferman's promise to its customers is to, "Deliver exceptional food experiences to our valued customers." You'll notice in that Wolferman's expresses its commitment to making its customers feel "delighted." I believe that if you exceed the customer's expectations you can succeed against the corporate goliaths. It's always great when someone responds to a request with, "It's my pleasure." Now that is the perfect promise signal and, hey, it works.

In order for a brand to be effective, it must be delivered at the "customer's convenience". In other words, if an organization promises to be fast or the most responsive, it must be perceived by the "essence" (heart, soul and the customers) just as fast. It doesn't matter if an organization is a family business, global corporation, nonprofit association, or a solo entrepreneur. The process is the same. If an entity has a good mission statement that explains what it does, then the mission statement can coexist with a promise that defines how an organization wants its customers to feel. Scott Smith of Haggen Food & Pharmacy describes this mindset from a customer's point of view, "I don't care how much you know until I know how much you care."

Based on the perceptual insights developed in a brand's research with consumers, customers, associates, and influencers, the goal is to address the following three questions, which were introduced. What is our experience all about? What distinguishes our products and services from competitors? What is superior about the value we offer our customers? However, in order to develop the right promise, an organization must adopt a customer-focused mindset.

For example, Costco has earned its own branded description for a great shopping experience called the "Costco Run." In Costco, there is a tendency for everyone to shop more than they planned, yet all wonder about how this could happen. Members' perception is confident about the Costco brand and that's the key as customers feel really good about trusting this super store. This is why its memberships increase at the rate of nearly eighty-seven percent year after year. Costco's commitment to its employees and members brings its promise to each customer.

The key questions are:

Does every person associated with a brand know what the promise is?

Does every associate know how he or she is supposed to deliver the promise?

Service means nothing unless it's connected to how a brand wants its customers to feel. A promise focuses on how an organization or individual wants its customers to feel, while missions or visions usually relate to what an organization expects to do. A genuine brand that has a real promise should know how its customers feel every day and not have to wait for a rating service to determine its customer satisfaction. So-called branding initiatives that do not include a real promise are a waste of time and money. The branding rule: "Treat customers better than they expect to be treated.

The "good brand" test:

- Can customers always talk to a real person?
- When customers talk to associates, do the associates make the customers feel that they are glad to help?
- Do associates sound positive and upbeat in order to lower customer anxiety levels?

AUTHORITY POSITIONING

You are an authority and an expert about something. Once you realize this, everything will fall into place. Ask yourself, what are you good at? What did you always dream to be? Have you always pictured yourself doing something in line with your interests? Knowledge is power, and when it comes to brand development, this is no exception.

Any successful brand must be good at its business, that is doing things right. However, building an optimum brand requires "doing the right things and living the authentic life." Genuine brands that dominate their segments always have a distinctive position in the consumer's mind and habitually create positive paradigm shifts that consumers enjoy. Time is listed first because it can be the source of tremendous competitive advantage. Everyone has a shortage of time, hence time is extremely valuable, and it is becoming a significant driver of perceived value. Genuine brands understand that their products and services are not simply a set of attributes or just a "thing." They understand that consumers are moved by the gestalt of the brand — all its tangible and intangible (functional and emotional) benefits, integrated into consumers' consciousness. Genuine brands deliver a distinctive promise that creates memorable value reaching far beyond their customer base. Any person or organization that wants to be a brand must focus on its promise to its customers, influencers, and employees. The widespread focus on "image" without the first requirement being a genuine promise is the real issue today, and I believe that this is one of the biggest challenges that traditional advertisers face. A brand is only as good or as valuable as it is. Imagine if every advertising agency required its clients to have a promise that their associates were delivering before creating any advertisement, promotion, or communication. Without a promise, a brand is at risk of failure.

Distinctive is the key word to understanding the real meaning of a brand. It's not an organization or company that gets to decide whether or not its brand is distinctive. A brand is distinctive only if its customers, consumers, associates, and influencers perceive and believe that it truly is. In order for an organization to become a genuine brand, several expectations must be met.

The more that you position yourself as an authority, the easier you will find it to attract your ideal tribe, as your clients will immediately see YOU as the "go to" person when they are looking to solve a problem that they have.

WHERE ARE YOU HEADED?

Once you know yourself better you can then figure out where you want to be later on. This is both for your personal and professional life. What life aspects have been rewarding?

Do you like the job you have currently or the business you are running? You may not like jobs you had in the past. However, there may have been periods in your life in which you were most happy. Use your memory to find life aspects that have been rewarding to you. Find aspects in both your personal and professional life that have been rewarding. Don't limit this list as you create it. List every positive thing until every life stage you have had has been assessed. Put each positive aspect into a category. Help narrow each category into a short list. You will soon see potential professions that will help your professional life become more satisfying. At this point, you will begin to see the profession type that makes you happiest.

The moment you determine where in life you want to be, compare these to your value list. You will most likely be excited about your career prospects and brand ideas at this point.

5 STEPS TO CREATE A COMPELLING COMPETITIVE ADVANTAGE THAT WILL MAKE YOUR BRAND STAND OUT

1. Find Your Market Strategic Position

What specific segment or niche in the market should be the focus of your company? Finding this has to do with combining business skills with the target prospect's unmet needs. You then need to design a service or product that fulfills this niche.

If you remember, the strategic position of Oprah in her Oprah Winfrey Show was "Own Your Power" — this is a great example of excellent personal branding.

2. Find Your Main BRAND

For differentiating you with your competitors, this is the most compelling advantage.

Tony Robbins utilized, "Awaken the Giant Within." This was the main advantage that addressed the needs of their market position that was newly defined — people who were achievers with a lot of potential but needed inspiration.

3. Find Your Supporting Business Model

Specifically, how will you be delivering what your Primary BRAND and Strategic Positioning promises? Your Supporting Business Model comprises features in your company that are needed to guarantee what you consistently deliver.

A model was built by Apple that delivered design that was extraordinary and a testing process that was rigorous and included the involvement of Steve Jobs.

A supporting model for business was built by Domino's to let them provide their promised advantages consistently, which was delivering your order in half an hour.

The business supporting model included locating a plain vanilla, low-cost pizzeria near schools and hiring staff for delivery, for instance.

4. Find Your Secondary BRAND

Zero-in on what you offer that no other business offers and which will help you stand out from the rest.

For Domino's, the benefits that are secondary could include a broader topping selection, extra-large slices or even great prices.

5. Making Your BRAND Statement

This is a simple two to three-line statement that you can do by combining steps one to four. Similar to a mission statement, this will identify what makes you different to your customers and target group.

Domino's slogan really sums up the Compelling Competitive Advantage of Domino's Pizza which is, "Delivered in thirty minutes or less or its FREE."

COMPETITIVE ADVANTAGES – #1 SERVICE

Everyone says that their service is outstanding but most don't really understand what makes them differentiated.

At this point I would like to focus on the six Value Added Service categories differentiating your business from the rest through the provision of high perceived values that will cost you next to nothing.

CONVENIENCE

In the hectic pace of life we live in, most people desire more time and not money. This is how 'convenience stores' have made their mark. Consumers happily pay twenty percent more for goods that are convenient. The food stores, coffee shops and gas station convenience stores are all examples of this.

Doing everything you can to make your product more convenient is a big step to creating a competitive advantage.

There are a few things you can do to make your business more convenient to your market:

Location — The best method of increasing convenience. It is not practical to change locations, of course. On the other hand, already having a good location is a good idea. Those found inside an industrial park location is definitely their main competitive advantage.

Mobile Services or Delivery — Bringing you service or product to consumers is the next best thing to location.

For example, there has been a proliferation of mechanics that are mobile since people don't really want to have to take their car to the shop. Also, in Sydney and Melbourne, there is an increased popularity in mobile dry cleaning.

Easy Ordering — It should not be too hard for consumers to order your products. For example, gourmet restaurants, Chinese food and diners tend to have ordering issues and don't even have online menus. This makes it hard to order compared to restaurants that give you easy ordering access.

Availability — Customers need to be able to do business with you even at odd hours. This is why twenty-four hour stores have been generating a lot of business. Of course I am not suggesting a drastic change, but rather to consider extending your operational hours to fit in with your customer's schedule.

Terms of Payment — You can make your company different by giving more options when it comes to terms of payment, such as offering payments that your customer can do in thirty, sixty or ninety day terms. Accepting credit cards is also a good idea.

Additional Services — Find out what your market perceives as important and offer it. For instance, having a play area for children in a clothing, furniture or computer shop so that parents can shop in peace is a good idea.

SPEED

It cannot be denied that needs of the customer are rapidly changing in our society, which is becoming more and more fast paced.

The emphasis on convenience and speed are becoming increasingly critical in their decisions of buying. For this reason, you need to have opportunities that are continuous for meeting these needs and for being able to develop into the dominant force in your industry.

If you are a publisher and can deliver job orders in twenty-four hours or less, then you are the only choice logical enough for those who would like their orders hurriedly delivered.

When supermarkets created an express line, this became a tremendous competitive advantage. Before this occurrence, just picking up eggs or a carton of milk was completely inconvenient since you had to stand in line behind someone with three full carts.

EDUCATION OR TRAINING

These categories symbolize two of the value-added services that are most powerful, especially if you are selling a type of commodity service or product where there is a requirement for knowledge or application.

One example is Bunnings, which has hired employees and has separated themselves from the competition through hiring former tradesmen and contractors. These people give advice on projects you undertake. They also offer classes to teach a variety of DIY building skills. If you need project guidance, Bunnings would be the choice logical for you.

Keep in mind that *Competitive Advantages are not just used for attracting brand new clientele but keeping the ones you already have.*

CREATING A RISK-FREE PURCHASE

Generous policy returns and guarantees are great as a tool for customer satisfaction. Also, they can be your strategic position. If none of the competition offers a money back guarantee of one hundred percent, then you have the chance to become the logical choice by doing this.

More than anything else, the one single thing that makes the shoe brand Zappos different, for example, is the generous policy of returns where they even offer to pay the cost of return shipping. Knowing this, why would customers purchase any other brand?

QUALITY

Properly defined, the nebulous term 'quality' can become a powerful competitive advantage. For our own purposes the definition of quality is: 'Which of the benefits perceived does the consumer get?'

For example, a pizzeria that features gourmet choices can differentiate itself easily from competitors that are lower in cost since this one offers only the highest grade ingredients.

How can you offer more convenience? What can you give that will make you stand out from the competition?

Questions to consider:
    How can you improve quality?
    How can you reduce the risk of buyers?
    How can you utilize training or education?
    How can you provide service that is faster?

How can you utilize selections to make you different from the competition without altering your business?

COMPETITIVE ADVANTAGES – #2 PRICING

I mentioned this earlier, and let me say this again. If you are just using price as your competitive advantage, you are going to make very low profits. On the other hand, if you use price as part of your positioning that is strategic but add other competitive advantages, then pricing becomes a tool that is quite powerful.

For instance, Bunnings has a wide selection of training and education as its plusses, then sums it up by saying: "lowest prices are just the beginning." This makes a hard-to-beat competitive advantage.

Using price as your competitive advantage falls into many classifications. These include levels of quality, service, lower prices, raising prices and price-fixing to reach various market segments.

Many times, people judge price and quality as one. For the purpose of repositioning products, businesses can actually raise their service or products to superior choices without altering anything else. High prices in themselves provide specific levels of higher perceived quality. In particular, this is true for items such as computers that most consumers don't know very much about.

Questions to consider:

How can you use price to make you different from your competitors?

Increase your level of service to raise prices?

Lower or raise your prices?

Give a fixed price?

For you to have a competitive advantage to become both actionable and marketable, you need to weld them into your BRAND or Competitive Advantage Statement. This is two or three descriptions of your sentence of what you do which differentiates you from the competitors.

Developing your statement includes both a primary and a secondary competitive advantage.

I would like to once again mention that you need to select competitive advantages that are easy to implement. This means that you don't need to close your business and start a new one. Rather, just incorporate these new concepts of Competitive Advantages into your normal routine.

5 STEPS FOR A WINNING COMPETITIVE ADVANTAGE STATEMENT

ONE: DETERMINE THE UNFULFILLED NEEDS OF YOUR CUSTOMERS

What is your opportunity to provide additional benefits and advantages to your target audience? What needs do they have that are unfulfilled?

Questions to consider:

Name one or two extra needs that you can fill now which will make you different from your competition?

What are one or two needs your customer has which you can fulfill?

TWO: DETERMINE YOUR CORE COMPETENCIES

To find out whether or not your competitive advantages are right for your business, you need to find out what you are good at. What are the core competencies of your company? What do you do well at the moment which your consumers praise you for?

Many times, enterprises seek something too big for their differentiation point. Get feedback from your customers that will let you know what compels them the most.

Questions to consider:

What are three competencies that will let your company provide the extra competitive advantage you want?

THREE: DETERMINE YOUR MAIN COMPETITIVE ADVANTAGES

Narrow down the lists of competitive advantages you know about your company into two main lists which you will make a focal point for the next thirty days. One is going to come from the advantages you currently have that exist and the other one is a new one. Your main competitive advantage represents these plusses that make you different from the competition at the topmost levels. For example, for Domino's it was "Delivery in 30 minutes or less or it's FREE."

Questions to consider:

Based on the last workshop, which compelling competitive advantages do you feel would affect your profits at the highest levels while being possible to apply?

Select one new competitive advantage you will integrate into your company that will be new to your business.

Select one competitive advantage that you have currently but do not communicate effectively to your target customers.

Next, transform those sentences into a one to two actionable sentence statement that will embody your marketplace differentiation.

FOUR: DETERMINE YOUR STATEMENT OF COMPETITIVE ADVANTAGE

This is important since you will be able to consistently and easily differentiate you from your target audience once you crystallize this.

What would you answer if someone inquired about what your company did? Being unable to answer this concisely and clearly means you won't be able to differentiate your business to your target audience effectively through communication.

5 ELEMENTS YOUR COMPELLING COMPETITIVE ADVANTAGE NEEDS TO CONTAIN

1. Be directed at your prospect targets.
2. Position you on top of the competition by listing one or two primary competitive advantages.
3. Describe your service or product.
4. List one or two secondary competitive advantages, such as your hours, that are extended.
5. Whenever possible, make the choice that is logical.

Using the sentence, "Do you know how…?" You want to identify the problem you need to solve. For instance:

"Do you know how hard it is to find someone to watch the kids so you can go to the gym?"

Next, follow this sentence with what your company can do and how you address the issue:

"Do you know how hard it is to find someone to watch the kids so you can go to the gym?"

"Well, I own a club for fitness that has a supervised play area for children aged two to eleven for women with small children."

This is indeed the logical choice a woman would make for choosing a place to work out, isn't it?

Now it's your turn to use the outlined method above. Of course, make modifications if you are creating a promotion piece or an ad, but the core message will be identical.

Begin with "Do you know…"

Explain "How you solve this problem and what you do."

Integrate the mentioned five elements: Be directed at your prospect targets, positioning yourself above the competition, describing your service or product, listing one or two advantages that are competitive, making a possible logical choice.

The secret is not to have more than three brief sentences and being concise whenever you can. It is of course all right if you are unable to crunch it down to two to three sentences.

FIVE: VALIDATE WHY SOMEONE WOULD VALUE YOUR PRIMARY COMPETITIVE ADVANTAGE

Validating your competitive advantage statement is important to your targeted prospects and customers. Here are some questions you need to answer:

What is the existing problem or market condition that supports your competitive advantage?

Will the benefits you state motivate them towards action?

Is it different from your competition?

Will they get what you promise?

Will your audience target perceive your advantages clearly?

YOUR BRAND LOGO

Since we are focusing on creating the advantage you have over the competition, your brand logo is important.

Your brand logo needs to address three points:

1. The strongest competitive advantage that differentiates you from
    the rest
2. Focusing on your target market
3. Defining your service or product

As their promotional driving force, Domino's used the "30 minutes
or It's Free" headline. This differentiated them from the competition
and made a deliverable claim by them.

Next, it also speaks to their target customers, who are people who
are busy and who value convenience and speed the most.

Third, it identifies the selling product clearly.

The center for fitness is another example. Traditional centers for
fitness could say, "Save twenty-five percent this summer at XYZ Fitness
Center, your complete fitness center."

On the other hand, a center for fitness with a headline that has a
competitive statement focuses on:

Defining your service or product: the health club

Focusing on your target customers with children and their mothers

The strongest competitive advantage is someone to watch the
children

"Take care of yourself. We'll take care of the kids."

"Our top grade health club focuses on the needs of moms and their
small kids."

Exercise

Write down two to three headlines and sub-headlines that you feel
will be motivation enough for your target customers. Make sure they
include the three discussed components:

Define the service or products

Focus on the target customers

The strongest competitive advantage that differentiates

In addition, your headlines can be focused on the problem of the
prospect or on the positive benefits. There are eight elements that your
brand promotion needs to include:

1. A self-serving, specific benefit headliner and sub-headliner or first paragraph
2. The specific outcome or benefit they will get (service or product features and benefits)
3. The reason why they need to purchase your item from you
4. The action you specifically need to take including terms and price
5. The specified action they need to make
6. A bonus or incentive that is compelling
7. How you will eliminate or minimize risk
8. The headline of the headlines which is your offer's key elements

Be sure to discuss all the relevant competitive advantages.

The script for the Fitness Club may be:

"Take Care of Yourself. We'll Take Care of the Kids."

Our top notch health club focuses on the needs of moms with small kids.

(Specifically, the self-serving headline benefits are: enabling women to work out)

Attempting to keep your commitment to a routine for working out is hard enough without being able to find someone to watch your kids every time. At XYZ Fitness we cater to moms with small kids aged two and up.

Two year-old Tommy and seven year-old Melinda's mom, Anne Johnson, says, "It is not possible to go to a health club three times a week if it wasn't for the children care center and activity center. The kids love it and I can work out in peace."

There is a complete staff for the kids' area from nine to seven pm daily and fun activities for kids of any age. There is even a computer and homework area for children!

Plus, special programs that include crafts and exercise are available for kids to enroll in.

Special workouts are also available for moms-to-be. (Special benefits they get and why they need to buy this from you).

There is also a fitness center that features a separate aerobics area so that you can work out in private. (Secondary features and competitive advantage)

Separate men and women whirlpools, saunas and the latest high-tech equipment.

There is also a professionally staffed yoga center where you can get beginners or advanced lessons.

Thirty-day trial free. Come bring your friends and their kids and experience the difference for an entire month. (Risk elimination)

The first fifty people who sign up, get a free trial and get a personal trainer provided for them for two hours in their free month. (Specific action and compelling offers to take)

Call us today, or just walk in to avail of your thirty-day trial free membership.

Here's to Your Health!

Mary Susan Jones
Program Director for Mothers
P.S. Those who bring their husbands can make this a whole family bonding experience as men get the opportunity to work out in exclusive areas made for men.

WORKSHOP
Draft an outline of your script with the template provided including the eight key elements.

When it comes to explaining the details of your business, keep it short rather than lengthy.

THE SUCCESS MODEL CHECK

It is vital that you check your brand and any of your ideas/products/systems through this model: Validity, Viability, Scalability, Sustainability, Duplicity.

What must people do to help their brand stay in the market and remain successful? There needs to be a brand check with regards to validating ideas, checking they are viable, scalability, sustainability and duplicity.

Validity
While some brands simply throw their programs out into the world to see whether or not it will click with the public, you need to validate and

test your product before its actual release. This does not mean that it won't get released. All it means is that you won't scratch your head later on and wonder why your product did not stick.

As a brand marketer, make sure that there are working programs that meet the objectives of your business. This is true for both entrepreneurs and small business owners. Continue to make sure that your brand meets business objectives.

Needless to say, validating your brand is part of the equation. This means you need to do an examination about whether or not your brand delivers on the set of goals you have set. The moment you establish what your brand embodies, and the type of emotional benefit it gives consumers, will help make sure you are on the right path. Use one-on-one interviews, attitude studies and perceptual maps that help you maintain the brand you are establishing.

Viability

In order for a brand to be viable, a brand developer needs to identify, develop, maintain, or enhance a brand's products' or services' distinctive characteristics. Distinction is a positive connotation, including special qualities, style, or attractiveness resulting in a perceptual difference in the nature or prominence of something.

When it comes to viability, a brand should be aspirational and invoke a positive feeling as well as a sense of pride. The brand development process should be focused on identifying, communicating, and delivering a brand's distinctive characteristics, those that are important to all its stakeholders and especially to its customers and prospective customers, while being beneficial to the customer. Distinctive characteristics must be apparent. The problem today is that many organizations' intended differentiation holds little meaning for customers. If a brand desires to be distinctive, there are endless possibilities and countless options. The secret is to select or develop distinctive attributes that customers and prospective customers will value most and prefer over other choices.

Value is not just price. Perceived value is the combination of customers' perception of the time involved and how they feel about a transaction and the price paid. Customers' perceived value generally has a lot to do with risk factors. Typical risks include customers' thoughts about what the competition has to offer and whether they are getting value for money.

Keep in mind that a key to success also involves the necessity for associates to feel that they are part of a brand's strategy and that they are passionate about delivering the promise. To be passionate about a promise is to believe in it and to desire to deliver it. However, it seems as though many organizations are possessed by policy-mania, that is, having a policy to control every possible occurrence. Organizational policies are obviously important, but only to the extent necessary. A merchandise return policy cannot by itself create the desired customer emotional perception. Empowered associates make the difference in delivering a brand's promise. One thing is for sure: if your organization, company, association, or nonprofit doesn't make a promise, then your associates may not know how they are supposed to make their customers or members feel.

The difficulty lies not so much in developing new ideas, as in escaping the old ones. The idea of keeping promises in terms of what your brand promises to offer is fundamental to our methodology. It's important to acknowledge that that's not always easy, but what could be more important? Imagine how different things would be if publicly-held companies voluntarily released their quarterly earnings with an independent report of their customer satisfaction scores. How about executive compensation plans that require exceptional customer satisfaction levels in order for workers to receive a bonus or stock-related benefits? These may seem like wild ideas. However, the paradigm shifts caused by eBay, Amazon.com, and others have occurred because consumers wanted a "better way" to shop. In fact, prior to the beginning of the internet retail craze, research indicated that over seventy-five percent of consumers wanted a better way to shop. Consumers love to be able to see whether sellers keep their promises before they buy in the new online world.

Ask your friends to share their recent exceptional experiences as a customer, and it's easy to understand why trust may not be the first thing that springs to mind when consumers think of certain products and services in the marketplace. You can trust the companies and organizations that make a promise and keep it. The goal of any organization should be to enhance its customers' lives.

Scalability

Your marketing strategy core is your brand. When your business happens to be in the growing mode, it is not hard to spotlight operations, which means keeping customers happy by delivering the product. Of course, it is critical to address operations. However, there is only so far that the company will experience growth this way. Begin at the foundation of your core in order to support the rest of your brand structure. When companies begin smaller and grow to become more complex, often, the market investments also grow proportionally to revenues. As your company grows, acquiring new clients becomes the priority. This can lead to a fast organization growth in such a way that the core values of your brand may be lost. When it comes to scalability, remember what got you growing in the first place.

It is particularly important in personal branding to be aware of scalability as many entrepreneurs get caught in the trap of developing products and services that are not able to be scaled on a large level. For example, with someone running a live workshop, there is only so many people you can put into one room, live, hence, a cap or limit on how big that product can grow. Always ask yourself: in order to create a truly scalable product, what can I develop, where I can sell one unit or one hundred thousand units, at the same time, without using any more of my time?

Sustainability

How long with your brand be around for? As long as you have a market for your brand, there will be a demand for it. The moment your brand stops being a benefit to others in terms of a service or product, this is the time your sales will see a decline. Sustain your product by knowing what the market needs and meeting every demand.

Brands that are sustainable are services and products with specified brands signifying extra added values in terms of social and environmental benefits to the clients, and thus enable being different from the competition.

Branding with sustainability in mind is the method of maintaining and creating a specific identity for a business, service or products reflecting extra additional value that the customer finds relevant. A brand with sustainability needs to have a culture that is integrated for success. The secret to a brand that is sustainable is trust between the brand and the consumer. Only when you achieve this can a brand be sustainable enough to truly reap the benefits of a unique selling proposition.

Your business is synonymous with your clients. One key aspect of success is when you enhance and maintain a good relationship with them. For future business and for referrals, preserving these relationships can be good for them as well as making the time spent on each project more satisfying and enjoyable. To foster important relationships in business, there are a few things you can do.

For example, asking questions will enable you to comprehend circumstances better. Take the time to inquire about what clients think and how they feel. With regards to the progress of your performance and the process, let them share their observations. When individuals take the time out to ask each other pertinent questions and learn about what interests them, you get to help make a good relationship even better.

To sustain successful relationships, it is important to have a clear contract. Knowing what your role is and what it is not will help set boundaries that automatically improve a relationship. Both you and the people you work with should know when the project is done and how success is to be measured. Once clients understand the role you play, the better they will tend to feel about you.

Focus on what you are supposed to deliver and what your contract stipulates. This is one great way to build and maintain the relationship you have with your client. When you truly deliver your project, you not only enhance your relationship but also build your credibility.

When you approach each project, use new approaches that you learn along the way. When you immediately find solutions because you assume every project is the same as the last one, this may turn off your client. Instead, realize that each situation has a nuance that makes it different from every other project. Take time to integrate them into your solution after inquiring thoroughly about them.

Sustaining a relationship is synonymous with sustaining your business. After all, it is your network of people, past clients, relationships and future clients that make a business thrive. For this reason, taking the time to create and apply methods to sustain business relationships will help you remain successful year after year.

Duplicity

It's important to think about how you are going to duplicate your brand from the beginning. Too many people who start brands or companies skip this step in the beginning and then they have challenges growing and developing in the future.

There are two options when it comes to your brand and growing your brand in the future. You can either duplicate yourself / your brand out, which means creating exact versions that function as a part of the larger whole, or, you can amplify yourself up.

A clear example of the duplication model is franchises. They take an exact replica of the business or brand that is working and recreate it to function in it's own right, using the exact same system as the original. An example of this is Subway. It started with one and duplicated the brand out through various stores throughout the world, all based off exactly the same brand and model.

The other option, is to amplify your brand up, which in one sense, ultimately means "celebritizing" yourself and growing your one brand bigger and bigger and bigger. Some good examples of this are Tony Robbins and Oprah. There is just one of them and they grow their brands bigger and bigger every year.

BUILDING YOUR LIST

Having a list of email addresses to market to is so important. Build your network through compiling a list to market by collecting emails, giving away freebies or even writing blog articles, among other things.

Why is developing your network or creating a list so crucial for your brand development effort? Network development or creating a list is essential for your efforts of brand development. Many companies launch a crowdfund campaign with the belief that the moment they sign up on one crowdfund platform, supporters will begin to flock to support them. They feel that all they need to do to develop a network would be to post their project. This could not be further from the truth. The fact is that you need to build your network systematically in order to effectively advertise your brand development campaign. This is where supporters like your family and friends come in. As a matter of fact, here are a few things you can do to build your network.

Ten Percent

In sales, there is a saying that one in ten people will be sure to make a purchase. In the world online, you will most likely need to gain even more than ten viewers to get one sale. Based on the rewards lists of your backers and your finance goal, you might need at least two hundred fifty backers. Being able to reach ten thousand people and finding methods of meeting this many potential financers is something you need to do. Look at businesses, blogs and organizations and see if there are any who would likely want to support your product or service and are aligned with the same values.

Talk

Discussing your plans with your network, family and friends, months before launching your brand development campaign will help build customer trust due to brand familiarity. In other words, people who have already heard of your product will feel more secure and will confidently offer support on the platform. Attending events and talking constantly about your product is going to help you get on the radar of the 'crowd' before they even see it online. This is also a great time to ask for connections and if anyone may know anyone in the media. If there are prominent communities you can reach that have to do with your product, now is the time to do that. Once you reach media outlets, this may be just the thing to boost your product's popularity with the crowd even further, causing your brand development campaign to potentially take off like a skyrocket.

Be Active

Based on how many people you want to reach, you might want to do research of the top bloggers that are related to your brand values and your product. It is important to become an online community member before you go ahead and put your project forward. Otherwise, why would anyone really give you a second thought? It is a good idea to be authentic. Speak to the people who are online with you. Think about what your brand values and product have in common with everyone else. Engage in topics that will bring your product up on the topic. In other words, to become successful at brand development for your project, your network is important. It can be the one thing that makes a difference of whether you make it or break it on the brand development platform.

How to Get More Online Reviews for Your Business

So you want to learn how to get more online reviews for your business. Whether your business is online or actual, or both, one thing for sure is that you won't be able to generate any positive reviews if your customers are not happy in the first place. If you have been in business for years and know for a fact that the reason for this is that customers do come back to get more of what you have to offer, now is the time to ask for some great reviews. To do this, put a link they can click on in your website or a sign in your store that shows them what to do to post a review.

A Word about Negative Reviews

Okay, a bad review is not exactly as bad as you might think it is. Yes, too many bad reviews can be a warning sign that there is an aspect of your business you need to amend, pay attention to or fix. At the same time, when you are offering great products coupled with great customer service, you will be sure to generate mostly good reviews and perhaps a couple of bad ones. It cannot be denied that in the world of online businesses, a bad review now and then is just a reality you and me will have to face. One benefit a bad review has is that when customers reading the reviews see that there are both bad and good reviews on the review page, they tend to trust the reviews more rather than when all the reviews look like it may have been "rigged," so to speak. When getting a bad review, remember to empathize with the customer, tell them you are sorry and respond to them thoughtfully. Offer them something that you hope will make up for their negative feelings, such as a promo or a freebie. This will be sure to keep them coming back.

Make it Easy

In your shop, one thing you can do to help customers leave reviews is set up a computer in one corner and have it ready for people to type in a few words. This is the best way to get great reviews with the least amount of effort on the part of either you or the customer. You can create a homepage on the Internet that features your profile and screensavers reminding customers to leave a good review.

Web Links

When you want customers to take action, one important element is simplicity. If you make it hard to find on a website where to click links, it is not going to happen. Rather, explain how much you appreciate a good review and make it easy for them to do. Have a devoted website section that makes it easy to navigate so that customers know where to go and what to do to leave a good word.

Email Signature Links

Many programs for email let you set up signatures for your email that show your contact information and valediction automatically whenever you send out mail. If this is something you have not already set up, then you should. It is a great method that automatically informs people already in your mailing list to send a good review. It can be something like, "Click Here If You Are a Happy Customer." This link should then send them your review site.

At Every Positive Interaction

Each and every time you interact positively with customers, ask for a review. Getting reviews for a business is not unlike making a sale. It just won't happen if you don't ask for it. This may sound like I am stating the obvious but really I am not. Remember to create goals for yourself and remember that each time a customer of yours has had a good business experience with you, ask for a review. If you meet the customer face to face, you can ask whether they are online or not. If so, then it shouldn't take too much more to ask for a good review. Explain that it is very easy to do it and that other clientele had not reviewed your site and that this is something important to you, which you totally appreciate. You might be surprised how many customers will be more than happy to do this.

ATTRACTING YOUR IDEAL TRIBE

The fastest way to get your brand seen and heard about is to establish what I call an 'obsessed tribe of people who just love you no matter what.'

Start asking your list / your tribe what it is that they want, what do they love about you, what do they want to see more of.

Step up and be their leader, they are looking for someone to follow.

If you don't give them an offer to follow you, join your list or eventually work with you, they're not going to come running out of nowhere and beg to do those things! YOU have to lead your tribe!

By getting very clear on who it is that you actually want to work with, you develop a filter, which also filters out the people who you don't want to work with, which is just as important!

Below is an exerpt from a small experience I had which may help you gain some clarity on how you can build your tribe so you end up with a community of people who you LOVE working with:

I'll never forget that phone call.

I'd agreed to jump on the phone with someone's partner to help them out with their mindset.

I'd been told that they were ready to change and wanted to invest in themselves to grow, they wanted ME, one-on-one, with no limits, weekly and DAILY access to ME and my coaching.

Cool, happy to chat.

Get past the small talk, then, two minutes in, I say,

"Now, _____ how can I really help you?"

And the response left me a little stunned…

"Well, Regan, if you're such a great coach then you should convince me as to why I should work with you."

Excuse me?

Convince?

Oh dear…

This isn't going to work out so well.

My response,

"Let me do you a favor.

There will be no convincing.

In fact, this conversation doesn't need to go any further.

Quite simply because, no offence, you're so far removed from the kind of person who I love to work with that it's ridiculous."

"Excuse me?"

"Sorry, did you not understand me?

You're just not the kind of person I work with.

Which, by the way, is totally FINE. However, this conversation doesn't need to go any further — there will be no convincing.

Although, if you ARE actually serious about working on yourself, I really recommend that you go and find someone who resonates with you, someone who you don't need to be 'convinced' into working with."

And that's where that conversation ended.

And MAN, it felt GOOD.

It felt SO good to have clarity.

And please understand, there is POWER in saying no.

Saying no to clients.

Saying no to money.

Saying no to working with someone who you KNOW is not your ideal tribe.

Because, I used to say yes.

And even if I KNEW it wasn't right, I'd twist and mold it until it appeared to fit in the moment…

And often it resulted in me not enjoying the process of working with that person.

SURE, I would get them results, yes… BUT if I wasn't enjoying it, then what the hell was the point?

I may have well just gone and got a highly-paid coaching job for a coaching firm that allocated clients where I didn't get a say in who I worked with. Same deal.

But that's not why I'm in business.

That's not why I built an empire.

That's certainly not what I preach to my tribe on a daily basis!

I believe that you get to choose.

I believe that you can choose not to help everyone.

Because deep down, not everyone WANTS your help!

It's like dating.

You don't just date everyone in sight.

You date who you are attracted to.

And you're either attracted to someone, or you're not.

Pretty simple really.

BUSINESS IS THE SAME.

You choose.

You choose your clients.

You choose your tribe.

Oh, what was that?

You're scared that if you get too "niched" (I hate that word — okay, too specific), you'll cut everyone out and you'll be left with NO ONE?

That, my friend, is your scarcity mindset trying to creep back in.

And quite honestly, I suggest you tap it quietly on it's head and ask it to please vacate the building…

Because it doesn't serve you.

ABUNDANCE, baby!

You get to choose!

And trust me, if you don't choose, you'll wind up sad and miserable, backed into a corner, working with people who you quite honestly just don't want to work with.

How do I know that?

BEEN THERE, DONE THAT!

But never again.

I love my tribe.

And they're so, EXACTLY, (almost scarily) down to a TEE, exactly who I want and love to work it.

They're go-getters, rock stars, creators who KNOW that doing the inner work is THE answer to having it all and they don't just talk about having it all, they ACTUALLY DO THE WORK to ensure that they are creating it all, on a daily basis.

So cheers to the crazy ones!

Action items:

1. Write down a description of your perfect target audience. Define your customers and prospects as narrowly as you can. What is their age and gender? Are they married, engaged, or single? Where do they live? What are their interests? What are their job titles? Where do they work? What do they talk about? If the answer to some of these questions is: "That doesn't matter," then that's okay. But try to paint as detailed a picture of who your customers are, and who you want them to be, as you can.

2. Once you've defined this audience, look for and find them on social networks. Dive into the Facebook advertising platform and see if you can determine how many people fit all of the criteria that you've written down. Search LinkedIn by job title or industry if you're in the B2B space. Search Twitter and Facebook for people talking about whatever it is that you think your customers talk about.

3. (A step to consider in the future after you have launched): Write down a list of places in your marketing budget where you're willing to invest in order to attract your ideal tribe. How could you potentially cut back from other marketing

and advertising expenses that are reaching a broader group in favor of more narrow targeting using social networks?

ESTABLISHING YOUR 12 MONTH PLAN

As stated earlier, branding takes up a relatively long period of time to attain the goal fully established. Long-term planning is very much required and needed for making that all-powerful brand; hence, brand value propositioning takes long to lay down the plan on the table, study the competitors, and propose term strategies.

However, if you follow this complete "Be Your Brand" system, you can develop and launch your personal brand easily within the first 60 days. Obviously if you are attending one of the Be Your Brand Online or Live Masterminds, your learning and your results will be accelerated.

To get your brand created in the right amount of time, create a twelve, nine, six, three, and one month plans including the steps and the deadline.

Focus on the development on the first month. Complete the three-month mark launch. Accelerate your progress after three months up to the twelfth month mark. Introduce new services and products within this time. Replace yourself completely out of the brand in twelve to twenty-four months. Here is a quick look in a summarized version of the timeline leading up to your brand:

- Twelve, Nine, Six, Three, One month plans, steps and deadlines.
- One month focus on development
- Three month mark launch complete
- Three to Twelve months accelerate + introduction of new products / services
- Twelve to Twenty-four months should be looking at completely replacing yourself out of the brand, apart from doing the things that you love

PERSONAL BRAND SUCCESS STORIES TO LEARN FROM

A successful individual who desires to build a celebrity brand must think like a "genuine celebrity brand," and this requires a different mindset, perspective, and strategy from business as usual. Successful individuals need to be perceived as distinctive and make a promise to deliver emotional and functional benefits. As Mark Steinberg says, "People try to create brands out of individuals who are not really committed to be a brand, and unfortunately, it's going to catch up with them." Mark should know; he is the senior vice president and global managing director of Golf for IMG, the sports and entertainment powerhouse. He also personally represents Tiger Woods and Annika Sorenstam. He also points out that to become a genuine celebrity brand requires a "promise and commitment to yourself, sport, work ethic, and character to become the person you want to be. When people think and act like a genuine celebrity brand, everyone who is associated with them understands what their promise is and how they deliver the right experience. Celebrities or successful individuals may be involved in a variety of business interests, and they must become actively involved in developing the strategy for their brand. It's important that each of those businesses and related brands deliver the right promise to their respective constituents. An individual's related enterprises must provide exceptional customer satisfaction for long-term success. The key for an individual to become a successful genuine brand is to focus on providing distinctive and relevant experiences that provide lasting and memorable impressions in all of his or her business-related activities. Genuine celebrity brands make a promise, and they deliver on that promise consistently, eagerly, and at the customer's convenience.

The power of a personal brand is based on how people feel toward the brand. Robert Tyrell Jones Jnr, popularly known as Bobby Jones, was one of the greatest golfers in the world. Clearly, his golf ability was world class; however, it was his demeanor and character that made him a genuine celebrity brand. Bobby Jones wrote the following in 1967 for the Augusta National Golf Club, "In golf, customs of etiquette and decorum are just as important as rules governing play. It is appropriate for spectators to applaud successful strokes in proportion to difficulty but excessive demonstrations by a player or his partisans are not proper because of the possible effect upon other competitors. Most distressing to those who love the game of golf is the applauding or cheering of misplays or misfortunes of a player. Such occurrences have been rare at the Masters, but we must eliminate them entirely if our patrons are to continue to merit their reputation as the most knowledgeable and considerate in the world." Bobby Jones' personal style made him distinctive in every way. Louise Suggs was one of the charter members of the Ladies Professional Golf Association (LPGA) that dominated women's golf in the late 1940s and throughout the 1950s with fifty-eight professional victories, including eleven major championships. Louise, who was nicknamed Little Miss Sluggs by Bob Hope, had the distinct pleasure of knowing Bobby Jones when she was learning to play golf.

She describes him as, "Always the Southern gentleman; he was an icon and not just in golf." She watched Bobby play a lot and it really helped her develop her style. Once he told Louise, "Knock the hell out of it, it will come down somewhere." When you listen to people who knew Bobby Jones, they always hold him in high esteem. It's easy to see why when you watch his golf instruction videos. His personal charm and sincerity were never overwhelmed by his intelligence or accomplishments. Many individuals become famous for their sports ability, acting talent, public service, politics, and the like. The few who achieve genuine brand status have demonstrated an understanding that to be perceived as truly "authentic" requires a unique mindset. It's not just about success, fame, or money; it's about achieving a balance between the fame and being perceived as a genuine person who is real and respected, not just some kind of a star.

Whether or not a famous person or an athlete can become a genuine celebrity brand depends on many factors. One of them being, is this person "brandable?" "You have to be good enough at something that someone really cares about," says Charlie Mechem, an esteemed corporate advisor and personal assistant to many celebrities, including Arnold Palmer and Annika Sorenstam. As the chairman emeritus of the Ladies Professional Golf Association, he has had a lot of firsthand experience in the celebrity business. If indeed people believe they are brandable, based on talent and accomplishments, then they will need to focus on becoming perceived as unique in a positive way.

There are so many talented people in every walk of life, being really good at what you do is only the entry fee. It is absolutely necessary to focus on your values, character and what you believe in. As Louise Suggs says, you have to have the right "basics" related to your talent as well as your personal life. Many famous people believe it's their right or obligation to tell other people how they should think, act, or behave. They say it's their right, as in free speech. Unfortunately, this is a serious problem, since there is no such thing as "free speech." The Constitution of the United States respects "freedom of speech" however, there are consequences whenever an individual speaks. People who desire to be genuine brands should always focus on being known for what they support in a positive way, rather than what they are against.

In order to become a genuine celebrity brand, a person needs to focus on being good enough at what he or she does so that other people will really care. The desire to be a genuine celebrity brand begins with the enthusiasm and excitement of a star combined with the grace and charm of a real person. BUILDING A PERSONAL BRAND IS HARD WORK. It's easy to admire celebrities' lifestyles and the benefits of being rich and famous, or both. However, successful celebrities' personal work schedules, social demands, and the nature of being famous add up to really hard work and lots of personal sacrifices.

GREG NORMAN

Mention the words "the shark," and many people will correctly think of Greg Norman. Although he became famous playing professional golf, his Great White Shark Enterprises provides a good lesson in how celebrities and famous athletes can build successful brands. He has consistently used the "shark" and shark-related images throughout his business to reinforce his brand equity. Greg Norman is actively involved in all of his brand ventures, and "he just has a really amazing business acumen," says Suzy Biszantz, CEO and president of the Greg Norman clothing line. "It's very natural to him. Our customers are always so surprised that, unlike many professional athletes, he's so in tune with our business and theirs."

Great White Shark Enterprises is a multinational corporation with hundreds of employees, partnerships, and licensing agreements. It is involved in golf course design, apparel, wines, and residential real estate development. According to Bryan Moss, president of Gulfstream (private jets), "He's one of those rare individuals where you can take his word or handshake to the bank." Greg Norman has been very successful in business and in the business of building his family of brands. He is involved in every aspect of his business, from tasting his wine to each detail of a development site. "My site visits are a little intense because I've got to see everything so I just put on my boots and go." In his book, *The Way of the Shark,* he tells the story of his friend teaching him the science of "DIN and DIP" — "Do It Now and Do It Proper." Even if you don't like doing something, you've got to do it anyway. He also believes in three principles: The next minute is the most important minute of your life. You are limited only by your own imagination. Your dreams are the blueprints of reality.

RACHAEL RAY

Rachael Ray — she's everywhere! Whether it's a bookstore, supermarket, or kitchen retailer, she's smiling at you from every corner. Her self-deprecating wit, appeal and hyper-energetic approach combine to make her a celebrity powerhouse. However, she did not get her celebrity status from a Hollywood plot, she earned it the old-fashioned way. Rachael was born in Cape Cod and grew up in the Adirondacks, working from the very start.

After failing to create food that sold well, she almost gave up, but her thirty-minute cooking classes persuaded local chefs to try them and she appeared at the TV station herself. The show was well-composed. They served a huge party and played theme music on camera.

She has become a chef that other people look up to and model — she has cookbooks that have millions published, and *The Rachael Ray Show*, co-produced by mentor Oprah Winfrey, has become a daytime hit. She's everywhere — providing for astronauts, and influencing corporate America to send many employees to cooking seminars in order to improve their management and interpersonal skills. As the *New York Times* reports, the cooking class approach to corporate team building has caught on. She isn't afraid to be real, and she loves having a fun favorite word. Here are a few recommendations for things to share from her magazine, *Every Day with Rachael Ray:* "Smiles with people passing on the street, time with someone who might be lonely, good thoughts with people you love, a great joke, your 300-plus thread count sheets." She works very hard, writing all her own recipes. Typical days start very early in the morning as she deals with endless interviews, photo shoots, and meetings. "I feel like an ox at the end of the day. I like working hard." It's easy to see why people connect with Rachael's personal warmth, sincerity, and never-ending energy. One thing that most successful celebrities have in common is that they love what they do, and they work hard. However, even working hard does not guarantee a successful brand. The key to building a genuine celebrity brand is to follow an authentic path such as this one.

KATHRYN AND CRAIG HALL

Many successful individuals have become involved in the wine business, but for Kathryn and Craig it is much more than another hobby: it's a real passion. Beginning with Sacrashe Vineyard in the Rutherford appellation of Napa Valley, they now own and manage over 3,300 acres with 500 acres being planted in vineyards. Their new Frank Gehry designed visitors' center for wine tasting, hospitality, and retail sales will serve as a focal point for creating a one-of-a-kind experience that "celebrates life." Craig and Kathryn Hall are collectors of contemporary art and greatly admire the work of Frank Gehry, believing it is art.

His sculptural approach to sculpture is best seen in his most famous work, the Guggenheim Museum in Spain, as well as the Walt Disney Concert Hall in Los Angeles. While they certainly are focused on growing and making fine wines, as Kathryn says, "We are in the wine business to inspire the senses and celebrate life." Everything they do is about creating an experience for others that fulfill that promise. Hopefully it's obvious by now that before a genuine celebrity brand can be developed, a very personal question must be answered: What's your promise?

Craig and Kathryn Hall would easily qualify as famous personal brands. Craig is a true self-made entrepreneur who started in business at the young age of ten to become the author of five books and the founder of a multi-billion dollar investment firm. And he received the Horatio Alger Award. Kathryn Hall was a successful corporate lawyer who acquired her interest in the wine business from her father, and she was the U.S. Ambassador to Austria from 1999 to 2001. Together they are developing their winery into a genuine brand that is destined to become a wine country landmark.

PART 2
LAUNCHING YOUR BRAND

Now that you are clear on who you are and your message that you want to shake the world with, we need to get into action and actually launch your brand! This section is all about how to launch your brand and get fast results!

It is so important to establish your brand and take action. You need to get this part right since this is your one shot opportunity to make it or break it.

When there are unwritten rules in launching a brand, going back to the basics is the smartest move to make. We can start by learning the fundamental marketing principles of branding, and adapting it to work for your own particular product and niche.

Let's start with the basics of naming a brand. What's in a name? Choosing a brand name is one of the most crucial factors that determine the success of a product. It can either help the product enhance its image among the target consumers, and eventually build a strong recall among them. On the Internet, however, the most popular brands have some of the most surprising names. For example: Yahoo!, one of the first search engines on the Internet, and Alibaba. com which is the most popular B2B (business to business site), are some good examples.

If you're confused about what your overall brand name would be, then you should probably just put down this book… YOUR NAME! The brand is you. The main brand name should be your full name and then you can develop further branded products and services under the main umbrella brand.

The fact is that it is from people that consumers buy from. For instance, a few years back there was one vendor I had the privilege of working with named Trent. He was a great guy and whenever we communicated for business there was a level of friendship, as well. Five years later? I can still tell you his name was Trent but not the company he worked for. Do you see my point? This is why it is best to use your own name as a brand.

Also, when you use your name for your brand, it makes it more than just a name and feels quite powerful. It is so much more than a label and gives you the feeling of creative freedom to create exactly the name you want. Rather than just a brand, there are no pre-existing near relatives in terms of style or design, so to speak. You will work to create great products when your name is on the label. It is both an expression of yourself and a reminder that you are indeed an achiever.

Check to see if your name brand is related to current trends and determine if this boxes you in. If you feel it does, then you might want to alter your style. Does the brand you have in mind already have a trademark? Also check to see if there are websites that already have your name. Do extensive research to see if there are similar names to yours and what products these are. Remember, it is a bad idea to rush the process. Stick to your timeline and ensure that you are hitting the target dates without having to urgently rush to maximize clear thinking. Does your brand name speak to your target market? If it does not then it should.

Now would also be a good time to begin developing a logo that is, yes, you got it — your name!

PROFESSIONAL PHOTOS

You've heard the saying: "A picture's worth a thousand words." When telling stories online, pictures and photographs are incredibly powerful tools. A huge reason for Facebook's explosive growth over the past five years is their addictive photo product as people naturally love to view and share photos that have been "tagged" to include themselves and their friends.

It is important for your branding that you ensure that you get professional photos taken that encapsulate you, who you are, your vibe and the image that you want to project out to the world.

PROFESSIONAL WEBSITE

Building brands online or building brands on the Internet has its many benefits. It costs a fraction of what companies usually spend on traditional media, like TV and radio. You also have a global reach through the Internet. This makes the playing field even for all companies, whether big or small. You can also measure the results of your efforts online easily and accurately by getting the statistics on how many people have simply logged on to your site. How long did they stay on your website? What are their reviews or testimonials about your products and services? These are usually the questions which can be easily gathered online from your clients and potential clients. The biggest advantage of building brands online is that it allows marketers to implement brand building at lightning speeds. It is very fast to implement, measure, and revise compared to traditional methods.

E-Marketing means you choose how you want to receive information with e-mail newsletters. You pick out which subscribe mode in which your Web and product should be marketed. This can be either in the classic mode or in the modern one. It is a matter of how brand builders and marketers will think of ways on making the virtual world of the Internet a customizable medium for their brand. For example, checking in a flight online conveniently, and paying bills online through the auto debit for your bank or paying your bills in that facility of your bank ATM are so convenient. These are the conveniences which will help you build your brand. Innovation plays a key role in this, obviously. By slowly adapting to the needs and wants of your customer and placing it to the Internet, this will automatically build your brand to the next level. It is a matter of establishing who you are, conveniently, efficiently, and convincingly. Firms nowadays have realized that, with consistency, brand identity can be foolproof. The era of similarity marketing has come and the influx of "me-too" products is forming a long queue in the market today. The challenge is becoming stiffer and stiffer. Loyalty among consumers is diminishing due to this fact.

Implementing differentiation strategies for products and services is being done by most brands today to create their own unique identity within its product category. Similar products do this by having a different approach in their advertising, product usage, and consumer promise. Aware of this problem, wise companies now see the need of making their brands speak directly to their target consumers by becoming free agents of the company. They have perceived the need for brands to have their own identity. According to David Aaker, in his book *Building Strong Brands* 1996, brand identity is a unique set of brand associations that the brand strategist aspires to create or maintain. These associations represent what the brand stands for and imply a promise to customers from the organization members. Identity, again, does not refer to the mere brand name of the product. It seems to spring from a single source, transmitted in terms of symbol and messages.

Market the products themselves with consistency. It is being as you are and following your own stable but individual plan that will get you far. Find out the real essence of the brand identity of a particular product and ask yourself:

- What is its individuality?
- What are its long-term goals and ambitions?
- What is its consistency?
- What are its values?
- What are its basic truths?
- What are its recognition signs?

These questions define what the brand is all about. It provides a basic framework that, when maximized and used faithfully in executing publicity and campaigns through the various communication channels/media, can help build up a strong, powerful brand in the long run. Here is the brand identity hexagon:

First, a brand has a physique, which is a mixture of independent characteristics that may either be prominent or dormant. Physique is the brand itself, it is the products of brand support. It derives its features from certain key elements or prominent features of the brand.

Second, a brand has personality. It acquires a character.

Third, the brand has its own culture from which every product thrives. Culture refers to the system of values, the source of inspiration and brand rendering of the brand. Many companies have neglected this and in short, have just concentrated on mere personality. It is only in recent years that this facet has been maximized in advertising campaigns, again to enhance the identity of the brand.

Fourth, a brand is a relationship. It provides opportunity for intangible exchange between persons, especially in the service sector.

Fifth, a brand reflects a customer's choices. It paints the person or personality of the consumer who will be utilizing the product.

Lastly, the brand identity is the customer's self-image. If reflection is the target's outward mirror, self-image is the target's own internal mirror. Our position toward a certain brand allows us to develop a certain type of inner relationship with ourselves.

Summarizing these facets of a brand identity, the identity prism drives us to one essential point about a brand: A brand has a voice. It is a "three dimensional entity" that can be maximized to enhance the credibility of a certain product or can even be sold by itself alone to the target buyers.

A Brand Value Proposition is the blueprint in which businesses create companies that define what a brand stands for and brand strategies. It is an enduring set of strategies and how it intends to win against its competitors. There are several advantages to a long-term brand value proposition. It permits companies to identify and develop strategies to own benefits on which category decisions are made. It creates a relevant and differentiated positioning based on an understanding of the overall category and the needs and interests of important segments. It creates organizational alignment because it is shared and understood by everyone within the company. It forces a disciplined approach in prioritizing allocation of resources. It drives messaging architecture, enabling communications to be structured and scripted to deliver a competitively advantaged belief system.

Branding nowadays is one of the most important things a company should take note of. Its strategies should be well planned. Its brand value should always be protected because it will set the product apart from the rest.

While brand identity is what a company works on to create a unique impression, the consumers, the brand image, is how the communication recipient per an entity is presented. It is how the public decodes the signals emitted by the brand through its products, services, and communication program. If the consumers interpret an image far off from what the brand wants to project, then there is work to be done. Of course, it is not purely what the company projects that penetrates the minds of the public. Extraneous factors are also playing a key role in either molding or damaging the image of a brand's positioning.

Again, brand positioning refers to the difference of a brand or product in mind. Belongingness reminds you that a brand or a product is nothing unless positioned in people's minds versus the competition.

BRAND POSITIONING

Knowing the right positioning for a brand in the public's mind is a very effective way of building that omni-powerful brand in the market. However, positioning a brand in the people's mind entails the use of media, and with the entrance of various media in our society today, communicating information to people, ironically, has become more and more difficult.

Influencing their minds, too, has been a greater challenge to people from any walk of life. All of these are due to the simple reason that certain things nowadays are over-communicated; hence, the mind is not able to cope.

Furthermore, in the over-communicated environment, people also tend to be more selective in accepting information. So another challenge for the marketing and advertising people is to capture or penetrate the three rings of defence of a person, namely:

1. The selective exposure;
2. The selective attention; and
3. The selective retention.

GOING GLOBAL

The important questions to ask when deciding whether to go online or global is whether it is desirable and is it feasible? The questions to ask whether to go global or not are:

Are you able to ship internationally without spending too much on cost? The differences in culture is another factor since each country has its own way of doing or making things. These include the differences in attitudes and the availability of media and exposure rates. The local marketing environment can also affect global brands since its name may be already used by many different companies. A number of products around the world have decided to go global in every sense of the word, but can all of them really be considered global brands? Why are Coca-Cola, McDonald's, and Marlboro, just to name a few, considered global brands? The answer is that they offer consumers across the globe a consistent (i.e. standardized) proposition and the same product formulation (Hankinson and Cowking, 1996). This is so because of the consistency of their brand propositions and product formulations across the world, which makes them global brands. It is this consistency that gives them the same reputation and personality, which establishes the same relationship with the local consumers everywhere. In reality, there are only a few global brands since other brands which are available globally would try to vary their proposition according to their market.

Nescafé, for example, has decided to individualize their products to meet the needs of their consumers.

A brand will only be recognized as a global brand if there is a single or standardized brand proposition and a standardized product formulation worldwide. The emergence of global brands has become more popular over the years due to improvements in communications. The growth of the travel industry has given rise to the growth of demographically similar consumers across the globe. Popular culture has a remarkable influence on fast food segments, music, fashion, and politics.

Companies today are shifting from the traditional brick-and-mortar stores to the brick-and-click stores. Selling online is growing at an unprecedented rate. This is the main challenge of going global, to grab a share in internet sales, where profit margins are higher. In establishing the global identity of a brand, it must seek the help of various communications media.

In the age of globalization, advertising, more than any other promotional activity, is about the creation and reinforcement of the brand proposition. Indeed, Ogilvy is quoted as saying that: "Every advertisement should be thought of as a contribution to the brand proposition." (Hankinson and Cowking, *The Communications Mix* 1996). Advertising, of all the elements, has perhaps responded fastest to the globalization of the marketing function, no doubt driven by the vast economies of the world which may be gained by standardizing messages and creative executions.

Aside from the traditional and non-traditional advertising, sponsorship can also be a vital medium, especially in global branding, by creating links between the sponsored event and the sponsoring brand such that the attributes and values of each become a shared resource. Global sponsorship usually focuses around two events, the Football World Cup and the Olympic Games. Public relations, on the other hand, aims to create a favorable reputation for the brand by influencing and coordinating different groups of people and different channels of communication. Unlike the other elements, public relations offers a considerable choice of communication channels like editorial, radio interviews, exhibitions, as well as new technologies like video news releases, and satellite conferencing, may be regarded as a continuous communication of the brand. Packaging many international brands, however, use different pack designs in different countries, sometimes resulting in adapted brand propositions and "local" design teams. Such practices lead to the communication of a consistent brand proposition through packaging unlikely. This has led many international companies and global borders to harmonize or standardize their pack designs across the world in its objective of converting products to sales.

Sales promotion is perhaps the most hard-nosed way of encouraging an intention to buy to a sale. Global campaigns are still in their infancy and often hampered by legal constraints which vary from country to country. Nevertheless, global campaigns can be successful when centrally coordinated and rolled out internationally with the minimum of regional adaptations.

And finally, direct marketing is increasingly being used to reach highly targeted segments of the international population on a personal, one-to-one basis. The aim of a marketing campaign is to establish and maintain a continuing, even life-long, relationship with a customer, either business or consumer.

Internet technology may be the most advanced communications medium today. However, this does not always equate to ease. Creating a brand on the Internet is just as hard as creating a brand outside the net. In fact, it is even harder to create one in this advanced medium. Plain advertising will not do the trick. The Internet, the fastest-growing platform today, is changing the way people live their lives in this no "off" age. The most prevalent misunderstanding of the Internet is the idea that advertising can be used to form online brands.

Several transformations have occurred to produce more effective online advertising:

Solutions over Benefits. Consumers are less interested in benefits, than in solutions to their problems.

Relationships over Transactions. Relationships between a brand and a commodity occur when a brand understands the consumer better than the consumer understands themself.

Dialogue over Monologue. Brands will both speak and listen. They will create e-mail programs, a destination site, as a community with opt-in personal links, offline marketing campaigns, and interactive opportunities.

Integration over Isolation. Consumers' messages must be integrated across all media

In a survey conducted by Greenfield Online for HMS Partners, it was found that there really is no direct relationship between ad spending and "top of mind" brand awareness for internet companies. The participants of this survey were asked to list only up to five names that come to mind when thinking about specific dot-com brands. It came as a surprise that some dot-com brands were able to have similar or greater levels of "top of mind" brand awareness despite having a smaller advertising budget compared to other big-spending brands. After all, who said the saying that it's not how much you spend, but how you spend it. Dot-coms know branding is crucial for success and most seem both willing and able to put considerable resources into supporting brands. The winners are going to be the ones that find the most effective ways and places to allocate those resources with effective online advertising. The best way to pull it off in the internet market is by doing a sequential campaign. Start off by using public relations as the primary key communication tool since, unless they are relatively known and already have some degree of presence in the mind of the people, advertising would just be a total waste of time and resources; and the fact that advertising needs the credibility and publicity that you can generate, integrated marketing has become more popular through the years.

Even with all the fanfare it's still all about using the launch of a program for advertising, publicity, and viral marketing techniques. What needs to be done to launch an impressive publicity campaign? After gaining some name identification and acceptance, shift to advertising to sustain it.

Internet brands have an advantage where communication with customers is short-lived. The Internet can provide better two-way communication with customers' real-world stores. But it can't provide a smile and a cup of coffee while someone shops. The question here is, are brands losing their personal touch if they become successful vendors online? Are people just buying online because of convenience and not because of brand loyalty?

Internet brands are still invisible until you type the brand name into the keyboard. If the person does not know the brand name and how to spell it, no sale happens. Therefore, online, name identification is paramount. Also, another important thing is, your brands featured on the website will be specific in order to deliver the needs and wants of the internet user by providing a well-constructed, updated, and beneficial website. This will keep them coming back. Traffic is built on your site, the branding strategies can kick in. Knowledge of a dot-com's brand in the consumer's mind does not mean he or she will join your community (your cybertribe), buy your product, or show you the kind of loyalty that will eventually turn into high, lifetime value. Branding is not something that must be taken lightly since it happens over time as a result of consistent efforts to communicate a clear message. Banner ads, even with flashing graphics and fabulous animation, never establish a brand and never will.

One master brand that has gotten it right on a global scale is IBM. In only a few short years, IBM has gone from what some would consider the heir to the grandfather's technology company to the inventor of the e-business dot-com.

While Barnes & Noble may have been the best-known bookseller on Earth, the first book store most people thought of was Amazon.com who was able to sell the e-pants off of them by creating a better concept. And because of the immediacy of the Internet, the value of Amazon's great concept could be spread around the globe in a matter of months. Today, Amazon.com is one of the most successful online vendors in the world. The Internet is transforming customer buying behavior, with major consequences for how the new breed of consumer develops familiarity with, and ultimate loyalty to the brand.

Marketers who strive to capitalize on these shifts, as all successful marketers must do, will have to better align their branding with new data about how consumers shop and buy online. Only by strategically recomposing the marketing mix can marketers drive traffic, build brand equity, and capture customer loyalty in the internet age.

J. G. Sandom, president of RappDigital, shares seven key secrets to successful branding on the Internet:

"Always start with a big idea, always.

For any given channel, leverage the medium that delivers the greatest return on investment against MarCom and business objectives.

There are real differences between online and offline brand attributes. In the offline universe, a brand is created by the advertiser and expressed through the media channel. The medium reveals the brand. The advertiser is in control.

In the online universe, the advertiser empowers the consumer to define an experience through which the brand is built. The medium creates the brand. The consumer is in control.

The Web has engendered a set of expectations inherent to the digital interactive medium, namely: speed, control, and value.

Maximize your use of creative assets across all media and geographies, preferably through an extranet-based asset management sys. Never forget to put language about global digital distribution.

Remember talent contracts. Don't be afraid to let ideas bubble up from their natural wellsprings."

Most of all, never forget that YOU should be the focus point and your product should speak to your target market. There needs to be converting. Find an industry expert to do this — send them examples of people's branding that you like and things you like about their website. Show credibility through testimonials and give access to products as well as services you are pre-launching. There needs to be the ability to opt into your mailing list, newsletter, or email updates.

As for pictures of your products, you have one go to get this done professionally! It's the most important thing and crucial for credibility.

WWW.YOURNAME.COM

Your website should be your name. Remember that people remember people, rather than companies. Plus, using your name encourages you to put your best foot forward. For this reason, you might want to buy various versions of misspellings of your own name as well, to avoid competition and confusion in the long run. Adapting to computer technology, whether you are well versed in technology or not, really isn't a choice these days. In other words, you have to.

The computer emerged into the scene around the 1940s. At that time, the impact of the computer created unlimited jobs for clerks. Peter Drucker (1979) pointed out that the computers, in spite of all the excitement and agitation they have been generating, were not yet economically significant. By far it was only used for clerical chores, which were unimportant by definition. During that time until the 1970s, people had not yet begun to exploit the full potential of the computers. It was only around the 1980s did it start to make great sense and significance. But now, we realize that the computer is more than just a machine that does arithmetic. It is only now that we begin to utilize the computer for the things it should be used: for information, control of manufacturing, control of inventory, shipments, deliveries, communication, and much more. If payrolls were all it could do, we would not be interested in it.

Ecommerce is the crystal ball in our fast-changing 'what worked yesterday probably does not work anymore' world. "The only permanent thing in this world is change," is such an undying cliché, but its truth is quite resounding. As we move further into the knowledge of basic assumptions, we soon find that the name of marketing and management, much of what was taught and practiced in the past, is becoming hopelessly out of date. Quite apparently, yesterday's basics are now the obsoletes or the archaic of today. Any marketer who does not decipher marketing trends will be even more flabbergasted in the future because new trends will alter the marketing realm. As a matter of fact, they are already in sight, and as they dominate the scene, they will compel us to modify most of the marketing strategies that have worked in the past. Quite frightening, but true, Alvin Toffler, author of *Future Shock* and *The Third Wave*, was on point in his theory on change. His discussion of the third wave has such a Nostradamus effect that it has become a concrete reality. "We are living through the greatest wave of change and enlightenment and the industrial revolution and waves cause the planet since the turbulence and buffering," says Toffer (MCB Business Strategy Publications). Although, often attributing it to technological change, Toffer stressed that this third wave of change is more than merely technological, it is a process of change altering cultures, social relationships, communications, and organizational structures.

Economists, political thinkers, and business leaders have yet to grasp the implications of this emerging society (Newell, 1997). Currently, consumer goods companies are looking at improving stronger relationships with their final consumers, in addition to the traditional business-to-business relationships with their immediate customers. Thus, all sectors — industrial services and consumers, are increasingly examining ways to develop greater competitive advantage through relationships-based strategies (Payne, 1995). They say that a new era of marketing has taken place. Out with the old and welcome the new! News, data information, and pictures have become even more mobile than people. They travel in "real time" — arriving at virtually the same time that they happen. And yonder the earth itself, the horizon of man has stretched out into stellar proportions. In marketing, there has now been a vicious and intensified shift from conventional to modern. Commerce and e-marketing have invaded the scene. Actually, there has been so much saturation already. The Internet is hot, and businesses are leaping on the surfboard into cyberspace. It is becoming a mainstream communications tool.

There is such a thing as merely using technology to sell your products versus using marketing principles in the process of understanding and meeting the needs of target consumers, and then employing integrated marketing programs to establish customer relationships in online businesses.

Can you imagine that Amazon.com, a company that sells books and CDs on the Internet, had annual sales of over eighteen billion USD? Jeff Bezos, the young mastermind behind the success of this service, understands that many consumers are willing to purchase books even without seeing them, as long as they are promoted properly. Bezos saw the power of the Internet in reaching a small, highly focused market segment, he realized that his comprehensive bookstore could not be all things to all people. For that reason, he established a sales associate program in which websites referring to a particular topic, such as public relations courses, could provide links to Amazon.com books that talk about public relations. To compensate the site, Amazon.com will remit a certain percentage of sales to it. The success of Amazon. com lies with the proper understanding of the needs and wants of the consumers, giving importance to the Four Ps and striving to improve each process continuously. Bezos, with his Amazon.com, serves as a very good example of success in e-marketing (Schneider and Perry, 1999). Because of the success of e-commerce, other such similar buzzwords have been coined in order to describe this phenomenon. Terms such as Web marketing.

Let's chat further on e-marketing online businesses. Which number is greater? The number of Web pages in the world or people? You guessed right. Web pages outnumber all the people on the planet. Taking into mind the simple statistic, simply having a Web presence isn't effective. First, yours has to be found among all the other webpages out there. And when someone comes to visit and visit again it has to be compelling enough. This is where the term "e-marketing" comes into play. E-marketing is marketing and promoting your website. It is developing and implementing a strategic plan that makes use of Web-specific promotion activities, as well as marketing techniques that are prevalent in "the real world."

In a continuously changing environment today, people must face greater challenges. A simple brick-and-mortar store can be transformed to a cyber-store engaged in e-commerce. But it does not end here. Because of the changes, good marketing programs have become more and more important to attain business success. That is why from e-commerce we can go to e-marketing.

As time passes, we will be overloaded with dot-com that will be turned to "dot-coma" for internet users. Competition will become tough in the cyberspace. Many people who engage in e-commerce would have the majority of the existing brand programs are just based on the assumption than on efficient data feedback. E-commerce is transacting commerce using the Internet; while e-marketing is marketing via the Net. E-commerce is plainly becoming the usual method for the transaction of commerce. However, to gain a competitive advantage, one must employ e-marketing. The key point is still satisfying online consumers and, finally, delighting them tying in the needs and wants of the client with quality service.

A brand is what identifies the product and differentiates it from its competitors. Building brand equity is important in ensuring the success of a product/service. Having a strong brand is one of the most important assets for a business to hold in the e-economy. Brand is very important because the customer cannot touch the product personally in order to buy it. Likewise, the company sales people do not have the chance to meet the buyer face-to-face. In the absence of these advantages, the buyer will often just rely on his "gut feel" and trust the brand or company that he thinks is reliable. Thus, the brand becomes the first thing that people search for in the e-environment of e-companies, therefore, it must come up with a strategic plan, as well as appropriate and effective marketing strategies in order to increase the awareness which places it in a different light. A brand can lose its value when it is forgettable.

For instance, Sony is very popular in making electronics such as televisions, etc. We recognize Sony as the number one main players, audio components in this product category. But what if they decide to sell laptops on the Net? Do you think it will have the same standing as when it sells its usual product line? The branding of a product will not necessarily transfer to another environment. Some experts have differentiated the emotional brand traditionally used in their other promotional efforts to uplift the image of their product. "Perhaps these types of branding can work in TRI-media (television, radio), and the use of ads are in a passive mode of information acceptance." (Schneider Perry, 2000). However, emotional appeals are hard to convey in the Internet. The main reason is because the Web is controlled mostly by the user. Many Web users are considered busy people so they probably don't have the time to buy into emotional appeals. Marketers are attempting to create and maintain brands on the Web by using "rational branding." Rational branding offers to help Web users to view an ad's emotional appeal.

Customer assistance, detailed product information, and personalized viewing of products are examples of strategies talking to the cognitive side of consumers. There are other strategies that can be employed in establishing brands on the Web aside from rational branding. Another method that can be used is a brand using an already established brand and extending the scope of its services or extension sales. Yahoo! is a perfect example of this. Aside from being one of the Web portal pioneers that provides a directory of websites, it developed one of the most successful search engines that allows any user to search information on the Web conveniently. It continues to take the lead by acquiring other businesses on the Web. In 1999, Yahoo! acquired Geocities and Broadcast.com, which entered into an extensive promotion partnership with a number of Fox entertainment and media companies. Yahoo! continues to lead its two nearest competitors, Excite and Infoseek, in ad revenue by adding features that Web users find useful and that increases the site's value to advertisers. Amazon.com's expansion from its original book business into CDs, videos, and auctions is another example of a website taking its dominant position and leveraging it by adding features useful to existing customers. The approach mentioned applies only to companies that have strong brand equity. But for new players in e-industry, it is a good move to employ affiliates where two companies and its affiliate partners are involved.

The Internet has changed the traditional way of the business part of the globe. Buyers can easily develop a relationship with you online and this is ideal. Prioritize getting the buyer's attention and building customers for every online business. Market fragmentation for the mass market is going into extinction and is being segmented further and further into smaller fragments, PR marketers creating products and services that communicate more specifically to smaller groups.

A very dedicated community is Multiply.com which is an eCircle for people who are active in posting pictures, blogs and music videos. In this community, a group of entrepreneurs are having a small businesses boom. Buying and selling just by displaying their products in their photo albums and offering courier services are part of their business. Members of this network are part of a growing market mostly composed of students to young professionals who have an active lifestyle and are very keen on the latest in fashion, technology, and the like. Multiply is being used by start-up entrepreneurs to market their products or services. The wide network of Multiply enables them to tap into their target market in a very cost-efficient way — it is basically free of charge!

Distant geographical boundaries are no more than technicalities when it comes to the Internet. There are no barriers to conducting business across nations and has made the factor of location less important which allows both buyers and marketers to circumvent several processes that could add cost and time in completing a business transaction. As with geography, time is also not a factor; a communication between businesses or individuals or both can be done in real time. Online stores never close and people can access them anytime they want regardless of their time zones. Knowledge Management (KM) sales reports, demographics, customers daily account information, and other valuable knowledge can be had, which can greatly help any business in their research.

Extensive customer service is important as well. This can include sending cards and greetings to develop a more personal relationship with their patrons. Also, newsletters and birthday greetings can be used for sending occasional promo announcements. An example under this category site is BirthdayAlarm. Sign up and the site will then send reminders to you via e-mail whenever a contact's birthday is near. Along with these reminders, there are free postcards which the user can send as a form of greeting. The site is not only limited to birthday greetings, it also sends greeting reminders and animated greetings for almost all occasions. The coordination Supply Chain Management (SCM) simply put, is to the customers.

Having an established distribution center also works. This allows to lower the costs of these processes and reduce the paper trail that sometimes causes delay and a lot of space. An example of this is the system being offered by a telecommunications company. This is an example of a business owner readily accessing different online inventory systems that can be installed in their company database to ease the function of inventory and order taking.

"I can blog, I can market" is what you need to tell yourself repeatedly as you get going marketing your brand. The Internet gives its users an immeasurable avenue to express themselves wherein the user can freely write his views toward a product or service. This gives the consumer an opportunity to liberally promote or go against a product which in a way is giving the user the power to market it.

Comments? Suggestions? Anyone? Most sites enable the user to post comments in a window that can either be displayed to the public or sometimes sent only to the administrator of the website. The consumer still has the power to immediately give his views on the products, which enables the company to address it. This works in many ways, quickly establishing the marketing, since it gives the company an opportunity to CRM by tackling the concerns of the consumers. A site which does have this feature for its registered user can sell products and advertise these for free. Not only that, but other people visiting the site may openly ask questions, write comments, and other sentiments about the product on the same piece for everyone to see.

A virtual store only in e-marketing. All the functions of a physical store such as inventory, display, and delivery are performed by online technology which is intangible. Hence, it is virtual, for it exists in a space that the user cannot see, yet the purpose of its tangible equivalent is still fulfilled. Aside from Amazon.com, another online marketplace is also seen in the form of eBay.com. At present, eBay is one of the top online shopping/selling sites wherein anyone who registers can sell or bid for almost anything, anywhere in the world. The different benefits of being on the Internet offer unique opportunities to businesses that are online.

On the flipside, since the competition is also amplified to a global scale, businesses have to work multitudes of times harder to get the attention of the consumer. The e-world is not just like the TV world wherein the marketer is fighting for the audience's attention through numerous ads and from different channels. The Internet is a much harder arena to fight for the user's attention, since here the user can just click the "x" on the window and the ad will be gone and there will be a very large possibility that the user won't see it again.

HAVING CONVERTING LANDING PAGES

When creating a landing page for products, use a separate website purely designed to pre-sell your first product (maybe a service, book, course, event, etc.). Make sure you have a high-converting video, about three to four minutes max. Ensure that each page is easy to navigate and that this takes them to payment page easily and quickly. Most of all, ensure that you have a high-converting copy that speaks to your target market. Promote one thing at a time — don't confuse people! Use a pop up box to grab their details if they go to click away from the site.

If you do not have landing pages that convert and take payments, then you are not a business, you are just a personality showing up online...

A WORD ON SOCIAL MEDIA

For social media, start with a Facebook-like page for your brand. This needs to be credible and needs to capture leads. Offer something for free in exchange for their email address. You can run Facebook-like campaigns to build up the list. I don't recommend buying a bunch of likes that are fake as they will not be your target and you won't have any luck marketing to them.

On Instagram, keep in mind that branded images are good, along with creative images about your brand / industry / product / service — make sure to be consistent to build followers.

On Twitter, start using periscope, if you don't already. Tweeting credible tweets about your product / brand / industry two to three times a day will get your brand far.

On LinkedIn, make sure your profile is up to date, professional and aligned with your new brand. Start networking with other people in your industry on here.

There are MANY other social media platforms out there and you should be showing up on a minimum of four. So ask yourself, where does my ideal tribe hang out online? And then make sure you have a strong presence there.

The social media revolution has given consumers around the world the most powerful voice they've ever had. It's also forced companies to think about how they can be more transparent and responsive. Social media, along with a global recession, has led companies, organizations, and governments to figure out how to accomplish more with less money, to get their messages out there and talked about, without spending as many dollars on declining media like television, radio, and print. Word-of-mouth marketing has always been considered the purest and best form of marketing, and social media has continued to prove this fact in many ways. People like to share with and feel connected to each other, brands, organizations, and even governments they like and trust.

Because of Facebook's 600 million users worldwide and more than 250 million mobile users, Facebook's Deals brings instant scale and credibility to the location check-in rewards business introduced by Foursquare and others. But there is no doubt that Facebook Deals will be a major force to be reckoned with. The potential impact of mobile and location-based social media cannot be overstated. For years, people have advocated the use of social media and a strong presence on social networks such as Facebook and Twitter as excellent brand-building and reputation-building tools. But the sales funnel through social networks is much longer. Instead of acquiring customers by acquiring likes, fans, and followers, engaging with them, and waiting to be there for them when they're ready to buy Facebook Deals, allow yourself to create a compelling offer and have it spread quickly through Facebook's powerful social graph with the virality of the News Feed. Facebook Deals allows you, to acquire new customers quickly through social networks.

LINKEDIN: FROM ONE PROFESSIONAL TO ANOTHER, TO 100 MILLION MORE, BEST USES: Recruitment, Retention, Industry Collaboration. You may not be the most organized professional on the planet. And I'll be the first to admit it, people have looked at my business card holder before and cringed. It's stuffed to the brim with cards, exploding out of every angle. This mess used to be my bible, one of the things I'd grab first if my office was on fire. Although you may always keep your business card book, it's quickly becoming irrelevant thanks to LinkedIn.

Facebook's Like button, introduced in April 2010, has already been added by more than 2 million distinct websites. The Like button allows Facebook's more than 600 million users, with one click, to express approval of companies, organizations, articles, or ideas. Whether it's a friend's picture of her baby you like, an article shared from the New York Times, a video from a local organization, or a contest from a global brand, the Like button gets more than one billion clicks per day. Yet as astounding as these numbers are, it's the new personalization of the Web that matters most in the social media revolution, both to companies and consumers. It's Facebook's ability to show you exactly what your friends and friends of friends like that makes the Like function such a powerful tool.

If you have a new baby, for example, you don't care what stroller is advertised on television, and, in fact, you probably don't care if 50, 500 or 5,000 people like a new stroller on Facebook. But if a friend of yours likes that stroller, you are more likely to feel that you can trust the company that made the item and are comfortable buying it.

Facebook isn't the only social network to adopt a "like" feature, either. YouTube, LinkedIn, and Foursquare have all added their own functionality that allows users to express approval of content, and Twitter has a Favorite button that allows users to approve of specific tweets. Content, companies, products, and ideas judged likeable by people you know and trust can be easily found throughout today's Internet. Companies and professionals who are worthy of people clicking their Like button will, in the short term, build trust and, in the long term, win the new Web in their respective categories.

Why don't you join the social media? Social media is like the world's largest cocktail party, where anyone can listen to others talking and join the conversation with anyone else about any topic of their choice. There are two main distinctions, though, between a real cocktail party and an online one: First, there's no drinking online, of course.

There are great stories and people who may bore you to death. Who do you want to see again or maybe even do business with at a cocktail party: the sales guy who talks incessantly about how great his company and products are or the person who listens to the problems you face, has an open discussion with you, and maybe even makes you laugh? We all intuitively know what makes some people at cocktail parties interesting and enjoyable to interact with. Yet most companies have not figured out how to be likeable in the cocktail party known as social media. Many companies still act like the sales guy who won't shut up about his products, or someone who tries too hard to dazzle people, or the person who bores everybody to death, talking without listening and not asking other people what they want to have a conversation about. The good news is, you, as a company, have an opportunity to do better, to be the organization that isn't that guy at the cocktail party. By applying the same set of rules you'd apply to be the person everyone wants to be involved with at the party, you can become the most likeable company or organization in your category — and end up the most profitable as well. Listen carefully, be transparent, be responsive, be authentic, tell great stories — the qualities that would make you the hotshot at the party — and they'll make your organization a likeable one on social networks.

But do you really want to trust your throbbing back to a complete stranger in an emergency? Then you think of another idea, and you head to Facebook and again search "back." At the top of the results is a doctor's listing with a sidebar telling you that three of your friends like this doctor. Beneath the top listing is a chiropractor, next to which you see two friends who like him. "Sweet," you think. "Someone I can trust, because my friends like him." You make a quick call, and you're off to get your backache taken care of by a recommended doctor, a professional your friends like. This scenario and scenarios such as this aren't happening en masse quite yet, but use of Facebook and the social graph (global mapping of people and how they're connected) for search and commerce isn't far off.

Think about it — why would you possibly make a decision about a doctor, an attorney, a mechanic, or any important product or service for that matter, based on advertising or Google placement when you can make this decision based on the preference and recommendations of trusted friends? Facebook and social media have made it infinitely easier to do the latter. It's nothing short of a game changer for marketers and businesses of all sizes.

The great news about the new world of communications we live in today is that everybody has a shot. Build a great product, get the word out to a few people, make it easy for people to share with their friends, and you can win without spending a boatload.

Just five years ago, for instance, if you went to a new restaurant that you loved, you might have shared the experience with a few of your friends, family, or neighbors. Perhaps if you really loved the restaurant, you raved about it for a week to as many as ten or fifteen friends. Today, you can share these thoughts with 200 Facebook friends, 300 Twitter followers, or 150 LinkedIn connections, all with one click on your computer or phone. No matter what the size of your business, organization, or client's business, you too have the ability to follow the simple rules of social media outlined in this book to reap the rewards.

Senior management, and anyone in a communications position for that matter, needs to know about social media marketing and how powerful or detrimental it can be.

Before we move on, I'd like to share three key points about social media to dispel any myths you may have heard and make sure I manage your expectations from the start:

1. Social media cannot make up for a bad product, company, or organization. If you're marketing a bad service or widget, not only will social media not help you, but it will actually hurt your

cause, as word will spread quickly. The good news is, if you're using social media well, you'll quickly know when you have bad products, employees, or processes. As a good businessperson or marketer, you can fix these problems before they cause any serious damage.

2. Social media won't lead to overnight sales success. We're talking about building relationships with people, and that invariably takes time

3. Social media is not free. It will take time and/or money to achieve sustained growth. Since it's free to join Facebook and any social network worth talking about, many marketers think social media is free, or at least cheap. Well, the good news is, no matter how large your company is, it's nearly impossible to spend the kind of money on social media that large companies regularly have spent on network television in the last twenty years. But building and executing a likeable social media plan will take lots of time and work.

Ultimately, such a plan can't be the sole effort of any one marketing or public relations department but instead must be integrated across your entire company, its agencies, and vendors.

BOOKS CAN BE SOCIAL, TOO. I write a lot in this book about the two-way interactive nature of social media and the importance of leveraging that potential. Of course, a book is typically as one-directional as a medium can be: author writes, and reader reads and digests. As a social media author, I simply won't allow that to be the case — so here's my promise to you: as you read this book, if you have any questions, need clarification, are uncertain about content, or want to challenge me on the points or strategies within, please do let me know, using social media.

INVITE YOUR TRIBE TO BE YOUR FIRST FANS

You've started a Facebook page and a Twitter account for your company. You've put up a YouTube channel, started a blog, and even added a button on your website promoting your Facebook page. You're doing everything you're supposed to do to "join the conversation" with social media. Yet up until now, the results have been dismal. You have a ridiculously low number of fans, considering the size of your business, and the only person you're having a conversation with is yourself. (Okay, maybe the guy in the cubicle next to you has joined in, too). But the promise of social media that you've heard so much about is far from being fulfilled. You don't know what you've done wrong or what you need to do to get on the right track to social network success.

Where are all of your Facebook fans?

Why isn't everyone giving you the "like" stamp of approval?

There's no reason to worry. No matter the size of your organization, gaining lots of fans on Facebook, followers on Twitter, and subscribers on your blog and YouTube is far from automatic. The bad news is that you're going to have to work for fans, friends, and followers, but the good news is that everyone else has to as well.

There are international brands that spend millions of dollars in marketing each year with fewer things on Facebook and no official Twitter presence at all, so the situation you're in right now puts you in good company for improvement.

Still, the Internet is nothing like it was even five years ago, where people endlessly surfed the Web. Many people just don't look information on the Web in that way anymore. If anything, they surf Facebook, Twitter, and other social networks looking for relevant and recommended content.

What that means for you, as a company, is that whether you're a huge brand or brand-new, people who don't know your product or service already are unlikely to be your first Facebook fans or Twitter followers. So who will become your first social media brand advocates?

Your strongest assets are customers, staff, partners, and vendors. However, to leverage this goodwill, you have to ask them to support the company through social networking and tell them why they should. Explain the benefits of social networking to your current supporters. Tell them why it is imperative that your company move forward with social media initiatives. Describe the ways their actions will help your company in your marketing and advertising efforts and make sure they understand how valuable their participation is in this process.

THE LIKE IS MORE IMPORTANT THAN THE LINK

Ten years ago, if you built a website for your company, you didn't expect thousands of strangers to just visit it, did you? Instead you used other marketing initiatives and assets to direct people to your website and spread the URL or link wherever you could. Sometimes people checked it out, and if they were interested in your content and trusted you enough, maybe they even stayed awhile or purchased your products and services.

Or if other related companies found your content useful, it was possible they linked their website to yours, in exchange for you linking back to them. This linking takes place in the hope of creating greater search engine optimization, and more website traffic.

Today, the "like" is more important than the "link." Getting people to your website may help them learn about your company and maybe even buy something, but getting them to like you on Facebook does two things that will contribute to long-term success.

First, when people use the Like function, they subscribe to your updates, allowing you to have a conversation with them on Facebook forever, unless you or they unsubscribe.

Second, it introduces and endorses you to every one of the user's friends. The average person on Facebook has 130 friends so with every "like," you're exposing your brand to another 130 potential customers, or more. Can you imagine if every time one individual visited your website, she shared that fact with 130 of her friends? ("Hey ladies, I just visited this site. Check it out, it's so great!") The same phenomenon is true for followers on Twitter, subscribers on YouTube or your blog, and other social networking outlets, but the numbers aren't as big as those on Facebook. Also, no network is as organically viral as Facebook's. Simply put, the more Likes content receives, the more often it will be viewed, and the number of people seeing and accessing the content will grow over time. There are long-lasting effects of the Like in Facebook search optimization: once you acquire a Like on your page, any of that person's friends will see this during future searches.

So if you're an attorney and one of your clients has "liked" you on Facebook, any time one of his friends searches for an attorney in the future and finds you, your client's testimonial ("Your friend John likes Bob the attorney") will be right there waiting for him.

If you represent a children's car-seat company, once one happy mommy customer "likes" your product on Facebook, her mom friends will quickly see her endorsement which proves to be more powerful than any advertisement.

HOW TO GET THE "LIKE"

How do you get people to actually "like" you? No matter well your brand is currently established, you'll need a proposition to your customers, staff, vendors, and partners regarding some sort of benefit they receive from your fans. Consider the following two different calls to action: you. Like us on Facebook now at Facebook.com/Brands versus Ask us your social media questions anytime at Facebook.com/Brands. The first one is totally brand-centric. Why would you possibly read that and decide to "like" our company unless you already knew us, loved us, and trusted us? The second call is consumer-centric and is likely to generate a lot more action, not only from people who already love us and trust us but also from casual first-time customers and maybe even prospects.

Did you know that you can't ask questions or post on a company's wall unless you already "like" it on Facebook? You probably hadn't thought about that, and neither did all of the people who just clicked the Like button in order to post their question. Whatever you can do to encourage activity on your Facebook page will in fact encourage Likes, without actually asking for them.

For instance, Oreo asks customers on their packaging: "To dunk or not to dunk? Let us know at Facebook.com/Oreo." They're encouraging people to share their opinions, and not just telling to "like" Oreo's online. More than 17 million people have "liked" the company on Facebook.

The value proposition might be different for each constituency. For example, you may want to invite your own staff to "like" your page with the incentive that they can post questions to the CEO, some of which will receive responses. For customers, however, you may invite them to access a discount surrounding people for joining you and then customers with that value proposition, or others at every opportunity, can be converted customers into fans, and that's where things begin to get interesting. Why should people "like" you on Facebook or follow you on Twitter? What's in it for them that's of value? How can you summarize that in a short, easy-to-understand call to action? The answer is, it depends on your business or organization.

Here are several real calls to action from clients to help you think about why people should like you:

Share your feedback with us at Facebook.com/VerizonFiOS.

Win prizes and join the conversation at Facebook.com/1800Flowers.

Free support quitting smoking at Facebook.com/NYCquits.

Connect with other moms like you at Facebook.com/striderite.

Join the conversation at Facebook.com/UnoChicagoGrill.

Get some at Facebook com/NYCcondom.

It's not about you, it's about your customers, and just like the Web quickly became too big to tell people to visit your website without telling them why, Facebook is too big to tell people to "like" you without telling them why — even your customers.

It's essential to develop that value proposition and then integrate it into your communications with customers and prospects. In essence, getting the "like" approval is essential for everyone but even more important for smaller businesses and new organizations which can utilize such free social media. Don't get anyone in your circle of influence to "like" you. Just don't do it without creating value for whoever the audience is. You're not going to get likes from anyone without giving him or her a valid reason. On the other hand, you're also not going to get "likes" from anyone without reminding him or her to "like" you. Give them value and opportunity, and your vendors, you. Your staff, and friends will join you. Where should you tell customers to "like" you? Provide potential followers and fans with value propositions to "like" you in as many places as possible.

Here are a number of places to consider integrating the call to action to your customers:

1. On your website.
2. On e-mail: send out as a company email.
3. On every staff person's e-mail signature.
4. On every business card handed out.
5. On every brochure you print.
6. On every receipt you hand out.
7. On every piece of snail mail you send out.
8. On every inbound phone call to your company.
9. On every outbound phone call from your company.
10. On packaging (as in the Oreo example).
11. On in-location signage.

Some of these more antiquated techniques, snail mail and brochures for example, are given new vitality and purpose both for you and your consumer if you can connect them directly to your online social network.

SALES NOW VS LIKE NOW

The typical e-commerce site features dozens, hundreds or thousands of products for sale, many of which are often pieces of text and graphics on such a site which have been carefully optimized to drive as many "clicks" to the cart as possible, attempting to maximize immediate sales. If that same e-commerce site were optimized for people to share what they "liked" by clicking the Like button on as many products or categories as possible? This function would create a permanent record of each visitor's interests. Then, friends of the visitors could go to the site, see the exact products their friend indicated he "liked", and could then buy it for him for a birthday, holiday or whatever reason. As a company, you'd get fewer immediate sales but you'd set yourself up to significantly increase your "conversion rate" (percentage of website visitors who buy your products or take further actions) in the future. Wouldn't you be more likely to buy something for your husband or your wife online if you saw he or she had already shown interest in it by "liking" it online?

Professional Services: Like as the New Referral Websites for doctors, dentists, lawyers, accountants, and other service professionals are set up now to convince you to call them — to take action now — but what if they were set up to generate Likes? If every professional took the time to say to all of their current clients, you are satisfied with our services and would like to let others know about your exceptional experience with our company, "please like us on Facebook," or "Ask us questions on our Facebook page," they'd instantly begin creating a valuable network, not only growing their exposure but also building a clientele who highly trusts them.

BRAND RECOGNITION AND BUILDING CREDIBILITY

You need to be seen on credible websites relevant to your industry — like CNN, Forbes, etc. Once you're featured in these media sites you can use those logos as credibility on your website. A press release is a good way to do this.

GETTING SEEN ONLINE

You could be the best coach, consultant or speaker in the world, for example, but if no one sees you and knows who you are, you are not going to have a big impact in this world. Getting seen online in this day and age is vital. Hire a SEO (Search Engine Optimization) professional, unless you're a computer expert that understands back links and how important it is to get SEO right. Your Google ranking and what comes up when people search your name is all CRUCIAL to your credibility and good SEO work will mean that your clients can find you easier.

ENSURE YOU BECOME A BEST SELLING AUTHOR

A best selling book is what you need to build credibility. Once you have established your brand and product, you might want to write a book and sell this on an online superstore. Ever wonder how to sell your book on Amazon? Amazon is a site that sells a variety of things users can buy such as health and beauty, apparel, kids' stuff, home and garden, electronics, digital downloads, games, movies, books and even groceries. How to make money selling on Amazon is easier than you think. Not only can surfers online buy these items brand new, some of the items can also be bought through individual sellers. If you want to capitalize on the high website traffic and name brand of Amazon in order to make some additional cash, there are a few ways you can sell absolutely anything.

When it comes to how to start selling your book on Amazon, the first thing you need to do is to sign up for an account on Amazon. If you are a first time user to this website, then providing the right information about yourself in terms of demographics is the first thing you need to do. Your login is automatically your email address.

Click on the button that says 'Your Account.' You will then see a 'My Seller Account' option. This link is something you need to choose so that you can create your own account as a seller. When someone buys an item that you are selling, Amazon can pay you through direct deposit. For this reason, you will need to set up a seller's account.

Select the link 'List Single Items for Sale.' This will take you to a website page that requests you to choose the category of your product where your item for sale is included. It will also ask you for your product's ASIN, UPC or ISBN number if this applies, along with the keyword or the title of the product. Click 'Continue' once the appropriate information is entered.

On Amazon, find products that match your item for sale. If it does not happen to be on sale at the moment in Amazon, you will see a message that says your item is ineligible for sale on Amazon Marketplace selling since it is not currently in the Amazon catalog. You will then need to describe your item's condition using categories that have been pre-set such as 'Collectible-Acceptable' or 'Used-Like New.' You can write a comment up to a thousand characters as well as the number of items you have before entering your item's price. Your zip code will then need to be entered so that buyers can see where their packages are getting shipped from.

As you begin your path of how to make money selling on Amazon, also click the link indicating whether you are willing to ship via expedited services or are able to ship internationally. Next, review your item for accuracy and click 'Submit Your Listing.' All you need to do now is promote your book, allow someone to buy your book and have them make a payment. This is how to make money selling on Amazon. Not only that, selling a book on Amazon solidifies you as an expert. For this reason, it is a good idea to start writing this straight away when you've developed your brand. Get it professionally edited. Decide whether to do it in hard copy or digital or both. Start getting your list and be excited about it being released. Launch it for $1 on Amazon and then increase price relative to the content and length of the book.

PART 3
ACCELERATING YOUR BRAND

Now you have developed and launched your personal brand and you're seeing incredible results, we need to crank it up. This section is all about how to grow and accelerate your results within your brand.

THE LITTLE THINGS MATTER

Many times it's the little extra things that matter the most. The truth is, a lot will depend on the specific nature of your brand and your online communities. One thing you can do once you decide to put your brand out there is "listen" to conversations that are not necessarily about your company and respond to questions that aren't directly aimed at you. Become part of these conversations and get involved in the community related to your company industry, but don't try to push your organization or a sales pitch onto consumers. This practice is particularly easy to do on Twitter, where conversation with strangers is the norm. So if you're a real estate agent, for example, you could listen for people asking questions about getting bank loans for down payments in your town and answer these questions with links to helpful online articles. Or if you're a local bed and breakfast, you might look for people asking questions about great vacation spots and recommend a few colleagues in exotic locations that you met at a trade show. You can provide unexpected value to people on Twitter and Facebook and expect nothing in return, you can create "wow" factors in different ways to promote yourself and your brand.

Promote moments that collectively will have impact on your business. Those vacation spots you recommended to others on Twitter will eventually have an opportunity to recommend you to their followers, for instance. Or if the articles you've supplied about loans are extremely helpful, these potential buyers may seek your assistance when purchasing a home.

Best Buy was the first large company to begin delivering unexpected value on Twitter in the form of answering people's questions. It developed the "Twelpforce," a group of nearly one thousand employees who were trained to respond to people's questions on Twitter about electronics products. When one of these hundreds of staff people aren't on the store floor helping an in-person customer, he or she is helping online customers and answering any questions about electronics products, including products not sold at Best Buy.

The big things matter, too, especially for larger organizations. Big things such as contests and sweepstakes can create "wow" moments, as they attract participants and winners. If you can create contests that bring people closer to your brand or strengthen that emotional connection, then they'll have long-lasting impact.

MAKING SELLING EASY

If you are not showing up and offering your community or your tribe products and services to buy, as we touched on in the last section of this book, you do not actually have a business. Now you have sales coming into your business, it's time to accelerate your sales and your results.

Facebook and other social networks have grown immensely in a few short years. By definition they are primarily social channels, not sales channels. However, that doesn't mean you can't use Facebook to directly sell, market, or grow your business. It does mean that the expectation most people have when they're on Facebook or another social network is that they are there to socialize and connect with others, not to shop. In order to effectively change a social network into a sales channel, you have to make the buying process as effortless and satisfying as possible. You also have to tread carefully: if you push too hard to market or sell, you will erode the all-important trust and likeability you've worked hard to achieve.

The big question on every marketer's mind is how to make money using social media. What is the real return on investment for all the time and money spent in the space. ROI forms, of course, brand and credibility, increased loyalty and frequency of purchase, recommendations, and decreased need for advertising, to name a few.

JUST BE YOU

A major paradigm-shift in marketing, media, and communications is well under way. Facebook and social networks are ushering in a new era marked by increased transparency and the most empowered consumers of all time. There is no doubt that this shift creates massive opportunities for the organizations that are most able to adapt their thinking and strategies to successfully implement plans via social media. All of the new social networking tools and sites can be overwhelming, and so-called experts, sharing opposing information or telling you to emphasize different priorities, make it even more challenging. In your company or organization, you're driven and measured by results. Since the results of leveraging social media are often not immediately apparent, it is tempting to rely on traditional marketing tactics that have proven to generate immediate results instead of utilizing social media. Resist that temptation.

Make good decisions about where and how to allocate your resources. And knowing the tools available through social media will make your job easier. But the process can be overwhelming. The contents of this book alone are likely difficult to digest and implement, so I suggest that when you first explore all the possibilities social media has to offer, you concentrate on these four key concepts: listen, be transparent, be responsive, and be likeable.

The biggest paradigm shift of all that social media represents is the ability to listen to what your customers and prospects are saying publicly. You can start listening today for free, and your ability to do so will inform and prepare you to best accomplish all of your social media marketing and advertising objectives. Acknowledging to your customers that you're listening can endear you to them forever. Before you talk, listen, and once you start talking, never stop listening. Transparency is the new default. People like when others are honest and transparent. You like when other people are honest and transparent. Yet somehow, so many companies and industries are secretive, even dishonest, about aspects of their business. Embrace transparency and openness. Be honest when you mess up and when things don't go as planned. The Internet becomes more transparent with every day that goes by. For you as a consumer, this is visibly beneficial, and it can also be a great thing for you as a marketer, if you can embrace it. Respond to everyone. The world is talking about you and to you. People everywhere are discussing their problems that you can solve better than your competitors. The world is telling you about their wants and needs that your organization can help them with.

Every time a customer or prospect talks publicly on a social network, it's an opportunity for you to respond and engage. When you don't respond, you either make a negative impression or you give a competitor an opportunity to reply. Every time you do respond, however, you have an opportunity to make a positive impression on customers, prospects, and on all of their friends.

Focus on just being "likeable." In the end, succeeding on social networks amounts to your ability to be likeable. There are two fundamental aspects to this term: likeable business practices and likeable content.

Adopting likeable business practices means treating customers the way you'd like to be treated. You need to follow the golden rule in each decision you make affecting your customers. Likeable content means you only share updates on Facebook or Twitter that would make you click the Like button if you were at the receiving end. Create and share stories, text, photos, videos, links, and applications that you as a consumer would want to "like," comment on, and "share." To be likeable, you must always respect and add value to your community.

One of the most fundamental decisions a company faces is its choice of market or markets to serve. Unfortunately, many firms enter markets with little thought as to their suitability for the firm. They are entered simply because they may be superficially attractive within a market for the firm's products or services. Without a doubt, a strong case can be made for choosing markets and industries where the prospects are attractive, and also where we can take a strong position. In general terms, the attractiveness of the markets and the strengths of the competitive positions we can take, will bring about several traps to be avoided.

Customers increasingly expect you to provide customer service and that expectation will only grow over time. You might consider using Twitter during live offline events or when hosting live chats. Twitter works well for conversations in which people want to address specific individuals and a general group at once. For example, if you are to tweet someone directly, addressing a message to one person's Twitter handle only this specific user will receive the tweet. If you use someone's Twitter handle in the text of a tweet, you are sending out to a group, for example congratulating a user, then both the entire group and the individual will receive the message. You can also use Twitter to host contests and promotions. Twitter can get quickly overwhelming to the novice user, so I suggest using a wide variety of applications to make your Twitter experience easier and richer.

UTLIZING DIRECT MESSAGES

These updates are private messages between accounts, similar to text messages. This comes in need to share or solicit private information, such as an account number or phone number. One of the distinctions of Facebook is that conversations are typically much more public. While people on Facebook mostly share with friends, no less than five percent of all Twitter users keep their updates private since most of them opt for all-inclusive, completely open conversations. Because of this, marketers are able to search conversations on Twitter and see all the conversations currently taking place. Twitter search is like the Google of conversation and provides insight to countless companies.

Before you even think about a social media strategy, you should head to Twitter to find out what your current social media presence actually is. Don't think you have one? Whether they're mentioning your brand by name or they're mentioning experiences related to using your brand, consumers are talking about interactions with your company or other companies like it and you need to know what they're saying before you begin your specific strategy. What words do people use when describing the problems your company solves? These are the words worth searching. Use "advanced search" to look only at specific geographic areas if only certain places apply to you. Twitter is also an incredible customer service tool. The main difference between Facebook and Twitter here is that you can, as a brand, send a direct message to someone who's following you on Twitter, while you can't on Facebook unless you're sending it from a personal profile. This situation troubles a lot of companies, but realize that this is to protect the Facebook user from being inundated with "spammy" messages from companies in their inbox.

UTILIZING ONLINE VIDEOS

Content is more important than product quality. A good flip cam will do or the camera on your phone. Short and sweet is almost always better. A good rule of thumb is to have fun. About thirty to ninety seconds per video is good. Video is a great way to showcase your brand's personality. Post it on YouTube and post video to Facebook. Don't just post to Vimeo and other sites. Consider using a service such as Tube Mogul to syndicate video across many sites. Make sure you are answering people's comments on social media. Just as you should be responsive on other social networks, so should you respond to people's comments and questions on YouTube. There is no better way to tell a story than through video, as evidenced by the rise of television advertising as the largest segment of the marketing and advertising industry by far (television accounts for more than thirty-two percent of all global advertising spending). Yet through YouTube, and other online video channels, your videos can be seen for a lot less money than what you would spend through traditional television advertising.

Are you a trusted advisor to your audience, creating valuable how-to videos?

Are you completely customer-focused, capturing video of users and allowing them to speak about your products or services?

Whoever you are, consider taking the things your brand fans love most about you and bringing them to life on YouTube.

Think about why you search online. It's usually because you want to know something — how to do something or where to find something. Consider creating videos that those questions relating to your products or customer experiences.

Also, forget the notion that YouTube is about creating "viral videos" getting millions of views. Is it possible to create videos on YouTube that will go viral? Sure.

EVERYBODY LOVES TO FEEL HEARD

Communication is fifty percent listening and fifty percent talking. Yet for many years, companies large and small have done a disproportionate amount of talking, shouting even. Customer service representatives, marketing researchers, and focus group organizers may listen, but budgets for these "listening" activities amount to little compared to the money spent on mass media "talking." For the first time in our history, now, through social media, companies can listen at scale to conversations about them and their competitors. You have a front seat to spontaneous chatter of interest to your business. You have the ability to check in on prospective customers or prospects discussing problems your company solves or listen to existing customers talk about unrelated issues just to get to know them better. Checking in on your vendors' partners, or even your competitors' customers has never been easier. The amount of data you can gather and the number of conversations you can tap into through social media is nothing short of mind-boggling.

As tempting as it may be to "join the conversation" on social networks, Facebook and Twitter simply aren't broadcast media. They're engagement media, or listening networks. Besides, how can you possibly know what to talk about in any conversation until you listen, at least a little bit? Ask anyone who has ever dated or been in a successful relationship how important it is not only to listen to your partner but to show him or her that you are truly listening. The guy on that first date who talks incessantly and does not listen strikes out every time. So does the woman at the cocktail party who only talks about herself. Increasingly, the same goes for the company that spends most of its marketing dollars talking and little time or money listening. Social media is the first communications channel that allows for such listening in large scale, and no matter what you sell or market, your customers are definitely talking. Listen first before you talk back. You can join the conversation as a listener.

THE BENEFITS OF LISTENING: WHY DOES IT REALLY MATTER?

If and when customers or prospects acknowledge that you're listening, you immediately strengthen your relationships with them. We'll talk more about responding later, but clearly the ability to not only listen but also to acknowledge others makes them feel heard, which makes them happier, which is always a good thing.

Even if you can't acknowledge customers (as is the case for highly regulated industries such as pharmaceutical and financial companies), in which only professionals can legally supply appropriate responses, if they can legally respond at all, there are other benefits to listening.

A better understanding of how your customers use your products or don't use them help you make critical changes to your offerings and information on how you communicate about them.

You can also uncover new opportunities you hadn't thought of or determine features you thought would be big hits that have ended up not mattering to customers, or being failures. Knowing what's important to your customers can help you better plan offers, promotions, and contests to further drive buzz and sales. Instead of expensive product launches, you can test new ideas carefully and receive feedback quickly, keeping yourself on the pulse of your customers. Avoid pricey ad campaigns championing things you think people will love about your product or service by listening to what people actually want.

LISTENING VERSUS MONITORING

Let's briefly compare the word-listening to the word-monitoring. A lot of companies and people use these words interchangeably to describe the process of seeing what people are saying about you, your products, and your competitors. Some may believe it is only a matter of semantics, but there is, in fact, an important distinction between the two. Monitoring has an impersonal feel to it, imparting a certain amount of creepiness. When you hear "monitoring," you most likely think of the FBI or surveillance cameras. You think of negative situations, "Monitor that cough, it might get worse." Listening, on the other hand, is an important human process, and I've yet to meet someone who doesn't like being listened to. Do you like being monitored? Do you like being listened to and heard?

HOW TO LISTEN

There are lots of free ways to listen to what customers and prospects are saying online, and there are many paid enterprise systems available as well, with costs ranging from a few dollars to thousands of dollars per month. If you're new to listening, try these free ways first: Google Alerts, Technorati blog search, Twitter search, Facebook search, YouTube search, Tweet Beep. If you go to any social network and type a phrase or keyword into its search function, you will see what people are saying using that keyword in real time. National and global brands might search the entire Web, while local and regional organizations will want to use geographical filtering to find posts only in their coverage area. Remember not just to search for your brand name but for your competitors and, more importantly, for terms and words that your customers would use.

For instance, if you're a real estate broker, sure, you can search social networks for the name of your agency. But wouldn't it be more helpful to search for the phrase "want to buy a house" in conversations on social networks in your town so you can find real people in real time sharing their needs with others? If you're an attorney, you can search for your firm's name, but it might be more helpful to search for the phrase "need to hire a lawyer" to listen to potential future clients talk about what they are looking for in the way of legal services.

For more advanced listeners, or for brands with higher volumes of conversations to listen to, consider a paid enterprise software solution. There are dozens of listening platforms available for you to choose from.

It simply doesn't make sense not to leverage the resources available to find out what your customers and prospects are saying and to use that information to create better products, services, and processes.

Whether your perfect target audience is one, ten, one hundred, one thousand, or one million people, you can now engage them in a way that was virtually impossible only a few years ago. Once you find your target audience, listen to them to find out what they are looking for, and provide your product or service to meet their needs. You build a relationship with this audience and, eventually, point them towards directly buying your goods or services, all using social media, the post, newspapers, magazines, television, and radio, allowing marketers to tap into wide audiences of people, based around demographic criteria.

ACCELERATING YOUR SOCIAL MEDIA AUDIENCES

Currently, millions of people are registered Facebook users. Facebook's ads aren't free to run, of course. This means that anyone who wants to, can easily research exactly how many people on Facebook fit into whatever targeting criteria he or she desires, free of charge. In other words, without even running any ads, you can find your target population among hundreds of millions of people simply by feeding Facebook the exact attributes you're looking for in an audience. The basics — gender, age, and location — allow you to quickly target millions of people on a large scale at once.

Change the way you would be using traditional media. (And before you tell me Facebook is solely for young people, note that in the United States alone there are more than twenty million users over age sixty). So, even though it's very general, if you're looking for your audience based only on age, gender, or location, you can certainly find it easily. It's the other categories, however, that allow you to drill deep down to identify your perfect audience. Let's focus on the two key targeting categories in this process: interests and workplace. In the "Interests" category, you can input literally any interest that at least 100 people have listed on their profile. Note: there are hundreds of thousands of options here. Type in "cooking," for instance, then more specifically, "Italian cooking," "Chinese cooking," or "French cooking." You could also go with "baking," then "baking pies" or "baking cakes." There are, of course, many possibilities and dozens of other cooking-related keywords. If you work in the food industry, these keywords are powerful search criteria in helping you find your target audience.

Searching for related words you decide to pick will depend on whether your products are meant for Italian cooking, if your company is a spice distributer for a chain of Chinese restaurants, or if you run a flour company, for instance. If you're a yoga center, consider targeting people nearby who list "yoga" as an interest. Perhaps you'd like to be more specific and target people who list "Bikram yoga" or "Reiki," depending on the services you offer or are researching to offer in the future. If you represent a nonprofit, consider targeting the thousands of people who list "philanthropy" as an interest. Then take it a step further, and check for specific causes that are relevant or reach out to other nonprofit workers who share a similar mission, locally or even globally. Also included in the "Interests" category is job title. Perhaps you want to target retail buyers, distributors, HR managers, journalists, doctors, dentists, or maybe CEOs. This search function is especially helpful in the B2B space. Remember, even in the B2B space, you're not marketing to businesses, you're marketing to people who happen to be decision makers for businesses — this is an important distinction.

We've grown our B2B business at Likeable significantly by targeting brand managers, CMOs, and marketing directors. For example, when we wanted to land an account with Neutrogena, we targeted marketing directors and managers at their company using Facebook ads. After we got their attention, they called us and became clients within a month. Two years later, the relationship is still going strong. In the "Workplace" category, you can input any workplace that multiple people on Facebook have identified as their employer. This function can actually be a helpful guide for local businesses that are geographically close to similar, larger companies.

We have a chiropractor client in San Francisco, for instance, who targets employees of nearby offices.

You can also use this function for the internal marketing and communications. Imagine telling the whole staff, "You're doing a great job, keep up the good work," just by sending out a Facebook message. Get creative with this function, and you'll figure out how to best utilize it for your organization

When you combine the "Job Title" category with "Workplace," then you can pinpoint your key audience with precision. Imagine, for instance, searching for only CEOs at Fortune 500 companies, or targeting real estate agents at the top five firms in town whether you're a small business, huge brand, nonprofit, or government agency, your perfect target audience will be found on Facebook. Frankly, I've yet to find an organization anywhere whose target audience isn't on Facebook. Be sure to listen, find, and engage your share of hundreds of millions of people across the world — the share that makes sense for your organization.

LINKEDIN: FOR MAXIMUM IMPACT, TARGET PROFESSIONALS ONLY

While Facebook may boast hundreds of millions of total users LinkedIn boasts tens of millions of professionals and business users. If you're in the business-to-business space, it's well worth looking at specific targeting options on LinkedIn. Such information provided includes the obvious, again, age, gender, and location — but also utilizes criteria that allow you to determine exactly who your audience should be, based on job title, industry, seniority, and company size. Software marketers might target information technology professionals. Financial planners might target C-level senior management in markets where they have offices.

We use LinkedIn to target senior marketing professionals in New York, Boston, and Chicago, the cities where we have offices. Also, the reality is, there are still some professionals, especially senior ones, who aren't on Facebook, and if you're going to find these folks at all online, LinkedIn is a great place to start.

FORGET DEMOGRAPHICS: TARGETING ON TWITTER

We've been talking about the amazing demographic targeting capabilities of Facebook and LinkedIn's ad platforms, but what about targeting people based on actual needs they have expressly shared? In other words, who cares about people's age or their job title or interests if you know that they are looking for a service or product you provide? You can find such people using Google, but the current leading platform for finding conversation is Twitter. All tweets are, by default, public. There is an immensely high volume of Tweets every day — more than ninety-five million. By utilizing Twitter, your target audience becomes based around what people are actually saying, not simply what you glean from demographic research.

Say, for instance, you're an entertainment lawyer, or you're in the marketing department for an entertainment law firm. You can target movie producers or actors or others you think might need your services. Or you can do a Twitter search. In this example, a search with the keywords "need entertainment lawyer" yields three people.

KNOW YOUR IDEAL TARGET AUDIENCE / YOUR IDEAL TRIBE

The last few decades have brought numerous improvements in marketing intelligence and research. But until now, you may have had no need to identify your target audience so narrowly. For example, you might know your audience loves playing sports, but perhaps they prefer one sport to another. Or young women love your product, but you didn't know that twenty-one to twenty-two year-olds are far more likely to buy it than twenty-three to twenty-four year-olds until you did the appropriate Facebook or Twitter searches. Now that you can target so precisely, you can always survey and research to learn exactly who the audience for your product and service actually is. While some businesses have narrower and more well-defined target audiences than others, you can always refine the notion of who is part of your ideal audience. You will likely find that there is more than just one group of people who are looking for your goods or services. Huge, global brands, for example, have certain categories of customers that are more common than others. Perhaps female lawyers spend more on your product than stay-at-home moms, for instance. If you don't know specifics, you can always ask, too. If you have 1,000 Facebook fans, ask what their favorite sport is. If you find out for some reason that nine out of ten of them prefer baseball, you might consider sponsoring a local little league team. Social media will help you find your target audience and provide you with further insight about this group.

PUT AN END TO WASTEFUL SPENDING

This is a common phrase about advertising among key marketing executives, "Fifty percent of my advertising works. I just don't know which fifty percent." Search marketing and social media have rendered it possible to target exactly the people you know are your customers and best prospects, not people you think are based on intuition and vague understanding of market research. You can continue to monitor your marketing and advertising dollars on less target-focus and awareness, or you can be narrower but much more potent. When tapping into that unique target audience, you'll never again want to waste precious marketing dollars on less accountable, out-of-focus media targeting.

This is just the beginning of the conversation, remember, we're not talking about advertising repeatedly in the hopes of eventually finding the right person at the right time who may happen to need to buy your product or service. We're talking about defining and finding the narrowly-targeted correct audience and then beginning to engage them in a conversation, so that when they are ready to buy, you're the obvious, logical choice. If you've targeted them correctly and then engaged with them along the way, when it comes time to buying, they won't even need to search, and they certainly won't need to respond to a television or radio ad. They'll already know you, trust you, and like you, so they'll turn right to you. And of course, you don't need to be peddling a physical product. Take, for example, Likeable's work with the Fibromyalgia & Fatigue Centers (FFC) and the steps we took in helping people afflicted with Fibromyalgia and Chronic Fatigue Syndrome and the F connect.

THINK AND ACT LIKE SOMEONE IN YOUR TRIBE WOULD

Do you like being disrupted? Do you enjoy when you're reading something online and a pop-up banner ad gets in the way of the next paragraph? What about when you're working on a project at the office, the phone rings, and you answer to find a sales guy on the other end of the line trying to pitch his wares?

When I speak at conferences, clubs, and meetings, I often tell my audiences, many of whom are marketers, to place themselves in the role of the consumer. I then ask, "How many of you listen to and enjoy radio commercials?" No hands. "How many of you watch and enjoy television commercials?" A couple of hands usually come up at this point, and normally, upon further review, these people are, in fact, ad guys. "How many of you use and enjoy Facebook? Here, hands shoot up in the air, anywhere between fifty percent and ninety percent of the room. Is this because Facebook, or social media as a whole, is the newest, shiniest product in town? I don't think so. I believe it's because people fundamentally want to use media for themselves, and connect with others, not to be interrupted.

Think about how you feel when you receive or experience the following: Direct mail magazine ads, TV ads, radio ads, packaging (i.e. "Free Toy Inside" on the cereal box), flyers handed to you on the street, billboards off the highway, automated messages when you're on hold, telling you to visit the company website, mobile/text messaging ads, ten minutes of ads before the trailers even start at the movie theater, e-mails constantly arriving in your inbox from marketing lists you don't remember signing up for, telemarketing and cold-calling to your home and office, advertisements and marketing ploys that are found just about everywhere we go. From the television in our living room to the stall in the public bathroom, from a drive down the interstate to a walk through the city's streets, from your phone line at work to your personal cell number: nowhere is safe from ads. And while some ads are funny, interesting, and even compelling, consider the consumer's viewpoint, you'll agree that most are simply disruptive and unwanted. So what's a marketer to do? How can you possibly avoid joining the endless parade of marketing and advertising disruptions in the quest to find your consumers? All you have to do is stop thinking like a marketer and start thinking like your consumer.

UNDERSTANDING WHAT YOUR TRIBE REALLY WANTS

With every Facebook message you send out, with every tweet you post, even with every e-mail or radio and television advertisement you write, ask yourself the following: Will the recipients of this message truly find it of value, or will they find it annoying and disruptive? Would you want to receive this message as a consumer? If you respond that, yes, as a consumer this message is of value and you would indeed want to receive it, then it is one worth communicating to your customers and the world. On the other hand, if you cannot see any true value to the consumer or you believe the message will only be an annoyance, then it's simply not worth sending. Why spend money, time, and effort only to contribute to mass advertising, marketing, and information noise that the consumer does not want or need in the first place? Sure, you might generate some Web traffic, phone calls, awareness, or even sales with any message, but you can run the risk of eroding your brand. Even if you generate sales from traditional, sales-heavy marketing messages and tactics, in the long run, the organizations that will win are the organizations that engage in positive, useful communications with their customers and prospects. Today, the most effective way to do so is to utilize the tools offered by social media.

1. How long ago was the content posted? In order to use this edge, you'll need to determine when your fans, friends and prospects are more likely to be logged on and using Facebook. Your customers are teenagers, for instance and you shouldn't share content during afternoons when they're at school. If you are targeting the nine-to-five office crowd, sharing content in the morning may be to your advantage, as many Facebook users in audience are likely to check their pages as they settle in at their desks. Your customers are mostly teachers, you'll want to share updates between three and five p.m. when they're likely working but not in front of their classes. In general, however, more users are logged in on weekend days, and since fewer companies are working then, weekends are the best time to share content.

2. Does this user interact with you often? If a user "liked" your page through a Facebook ad but never visited that page and didn't have friends who interacted with your page, the user is

much less likely to see any of your content updates. If the user visits your page from time to time, has liked the occasional post, or has even viewed photos from your company, your chances of showing up in his or her news feed increase dramatically. Keep this setup in mind, as this is why getting likes initially on your content is so very important — once you get someone engaged, a dialogue between you and the consumer or prospect is created, one that can be built upon and continued

3. How interactive are the engagements with the post? This edge is the simplest and most worth focusing on. Facebook's algorithm determines the level of interest or relevancy of an object based on the number of comments and likes it receives. The greater the response to the object, the more likely it is to show up in users' News Feeds. Of course, this is a powerful content cyclical concept: if a Facebook topic receives enough comments and likes, it will rise to the users' News Feeds, where it will be more likely to generate an even greater number of responses. If, on the other hand, the content doesn't quickly catch on, it won't rise to the top of users' news feeds and will remain virtually invisible. Have you ever heard of Edge Rank? If you haven't, then you need to read closely.

HOW TO MAKE EDGE RANK WORK FOR YOU

Facebook's News Feed algorithm is nothing short of revolutionary. Imagine if television commercials people didn't want to watch disappeared or if direct mail that the first few recipients didn't open stopped being sent out, never making it to your door. Consider how much you would pay to have e-mails people didn't respond to positively remain out of your inbox. Facebook has effectively created a system that filters out all the junk the user couldn't care less about or, worse yet, will respond to negatively. This situation forces companies, and individuals, to think incredibly carefully about the content they share — it's a great thing for users and a powerful tool for marketers and advertisers who understand what their consumers want and don't want.

Let's look at an example. Conglomerate A is a global sneaker brand that has spent millions of dollars in advertising to grow a Facebook fan base of one million fans. Your similar, though much smaller, organization has far fewer resources and currently has only 5,000 fans, half of whom happen to also be fans of Conglomerate A. Conglomerate A shares a traditional marketing message with its fans, "Check out our new running shoes on our website and buy them now!" Only a handful of people click the Like button or comment on the content. Since the company has failed to engage its audience, only a few hundred people will end up seeing the update, as it will not be moved up into users' "Top News" feeds. Your company, however, shares a link to your website with the following update at the same time as Conglomerate A's "Click 'Like' if you're excited about the weekend! Anybody going running?" Here, you attempt to engage the user with a more personalized, friendly, and less demanding message. You are not just telling them to "go buy shoes." Your update then generates comments and likes, enough to stay at the top of thousands of people's News Feeds for a day. This placement, in turn, generates greater clicks and higher sales. More importantly, the comments left lead to a conversation that will aid your success in the next update you share. You've outdone Conglomerate A; while it was busy marketing, you were thinking like your consumers, engaging them, and building an invaluable audience.

UNDERSTANDING WHAT YOUR TRIBE LOVES

The important question is, what do your consumers truly want? Consider what they care about. What do they value? What content will get them to authentically click "like" and increase your visibility among users? Mind you can't just keep sharing updates asking people to like the content, as that would quickly get as annoying and disruptive as many of the traditional marketing tactics you've grown to know and hate. For the answers, look to what you already know about, and if you don't know something, ask!

Consumers, for instance, say you have a male-focused customer base. You suspect these consumers are big sports fans, but you're not sure what sports or teams they are most interested in. You could simply ask on Facebook, "What's your favorite major sporting event of the year? Who did you root for this past season?" If your fans overwhelmingly say the Super Bowl and provide their favorite football teams, you'll want to share content about the sport in the future, even if your product has nothing to do with football. If you were your consumer, what would make you click Like or leave a comment? An appetizing photo? A funny video? The fact that nobody knew about you? One thing users are sure not to respond to positively is a press release about your latest earnings statement, new hire, or new product. There may be an audience who cares enough about this information to warrant sharing it elsewhere, but that audience is not the group to target on Facebook. The Facebook audience doesn't care. Facebook, Twitter, and all social networks are not broadcast media — I can't stress this enough — engage, don't broadcast!

Action Items:
1. Write down what your typical customer likes. Try to avoid writing things your customer likes about your company or products and instead focus on their interests. What sort of content would make you click the Like button if you saw it as consumer friendly? Write down ten examples of such likeable content.
2. Take messaging that your organization has used in written marketing materials in the past and rewrite it for the social Web, making the material more valuable or interesting to the audience. It should be short and sweet, and something you'd want to receive if you were the consumer, not something you have wanted to send as the marketer.
3. Create a plan for how you might create valued content not just for social networks, but for all marketing and communications content. What would you change in your e-mail marketing, direct mail, Web content, and ad copy if you thought like your consumer instead of a marketer? Can you create better content in all of your communication?

ENGAGING YOUR TRIBE

So what does "being engaged" really mean? To be engaged means to be genuinely interested in what your customers have to say. You have to want, even crave, feedback of all kinds because you know it gives you important data to build a better organization. Each individual at your company has to provide his or her full attention, mind, and energy with the customer or task at hand while maintaining the mission and core values of the organization. Anyone can send out an e-mail or a Facebook or Twitter message, but it takes commitment and focus to actually connect with people. You simply can't "be engaged" on the social Web because it's "the thing to do" now, or you read about it in a book, or you think it will lead to increased sales. You have to authentically believe that being active in growing your social network will lead to deeper, stronger relationships with your customers. You have to be interested in your consumers and prospects, and the creation of a solid bond with them must be your goal.

GET BACK TO YOUR CORE VALUES

Most companies, at least when they are first formed, have the best of intentions. Many times, the entrepreneurs' original motive is to create a solution in an attempt to solve a problem. Companies don't necessarily start off seeing people as signs or statistics. But as organizations grow, they get hard to manage. It becomes easy to lose the initial mind-set of authentically wanting to be there and fully present for your customer and even easier to drift away from your fundamentals and core values.

What is your organization like now?

Are you the kind of company that truly cares about its customers and values feedback?

Does the marketing arm of your organization act more like an old professor at a large university lecture or like a young interested teaching assistant leading a group into discovery and learning together? It may be hard to honestly and accurately assess yourself and your company, but it's imperative if you plan to survive in the social media age, in which a direct relationship with your customers is becoming the only way to succeed.

If your organization looks like the tired, old professor, the good news is that you're certainly not alone. The bad news is that it's a going to take a lot of work and a commitment from senior management in order to get the company seriously engaged with its constituents and return to the core values of simply being a business catering to the consumers' wants, needs, and desires. You can certainly follow the rules to look more engaged, but until you are more engaged, you run the risk of being known as only feigning interest in your consumer base.

BUILDING TRIBES AND COMMUNITIES AROUND TRUST AND LOYALTY

When you make the commitment to listen to and engage with your customers and prospects, it fosters a genuine sense of trust and loyalty between you and them, and among themselves.

Think about the university analogy: In a large lecture, how comfortable would you feel disagreeing with the professor in front of the whole class? How would you feel being the second person to speak up, after someone with a dissenting opinion talks? You probably wouldn't feel very comfortable speaking up at all, and neither would others, which is why day after day in that lecture, the professor talks, and students listen and take notes. This setup doesn't really facilitate a valuable relationship or learning experience.

However, if in a smaller discussion class the instructor makes it clear on the first day that the atmosphere is one in which all opinions and comments are respected, where dialogue and dissent is welcomed and even encouraged, and where the teacher hopes to demonstrate that she wants to be as interested in what everyone has to say as they are interested in her, it fosters a community based around respect and trust. This teacher, whether he's a TA, grad student, or full-time professor is seeking to create a discussion, not just lecture at the audience. Students will feel much safer and more empowered to speak up. They may also continue the dialogue without the instructor and beyond class time.

That second class is building a community with value far beyond what the professor may have provided solely, by way of imparting knowledge. If you can similarly build and engage an authentic community in this way, your community will bring your brand value beyond what you may see right now. Engaging your customers or prospects and getting them involved in your brand community will create a sense of trust and loyalty between you and your customers. An authentic, engaged brand community can live anywhere online, on a blog, through Twitter, or on YouTube, for instance. However, most brand communities are on Facebook pages, the predominant social media site. Brand communities are usually started by companies but, take off, almost taking on a life of their own when customers join the conversation. How well you talk to your customers matters. After all, they trust and value you.

CUSTOMERS SOLVING CUSTOMER SERVICE ISSUES

One example of the benefits of building an engaged community is that customers will help one another out. If you create a place on Facebook or Twitter for people to ask questions, share feedback, and interact with not only you but one another, you will engender trust and loyalty and help the community grow. Customers or prospects will take notice and appreciate when you answer questions on a timely basis and in an authentic way. If you provide a place for consumers to connect and to gripe, to share information and to learn and to grow, people will realize you are committed to them and the community you are fostering, and they will return that commitment to you. So now when someone unfamiliar with your company comes to the community, a potentially huge new prospect, and posts a question, another member of the community might answer the prospect's question before you have time to.

Or when an unsatisfied customer comes to the Facebook page to complain, the community is likely to rally behind you without you even having to ask.

How valuable might each of those things be to the bottom line? An engaged community grows your stakeholders in the company way beyond the staff and shareholders. These stakeholders will show support for you throughout their online social network and beyond. Your company's reputation and visibility will grow, and in return, your online and offline community will flourish.

DEALING WITH "NEGATIVE" PUBLIC COMMENTS

You've worked hard for months with your team on social media and incorporated the best practices and planned social media into your business. You've built a Facebook page, blog, and you're excited to join the age, a Twitter account, and an online conversation to foster a burgeoning community. Several coworkers have rallied behind you, supporting the importance of engaging customers throughout every step of their relationship with your company.

Then, the night before the big launch day, you receive a phone call from your frantic chief executive officer. Remind me, what on earth are we going to do if people write bad things about us on our Facebook page? We can delete those, right? Because if we can't delete those negative comments, I don't think we're ready for Facebook. Be prepared to answer every type of comment, both negative and positive.

EMBRACE WHAT YOU CAN'T CONTROL

Remember those comment cards every business used to have with a box you could drop them in? Many small businesses and restaurants still have them today. Whether your company officially has comment cards or not, they exist in Facebook, Twitter, blogs, and other online social outlets.

The good news for the customer is that the today's consumer base is the most empowered in history. If you have a negative experience with any company or professional, you can fill out "a comment card" from your smart phone that instant and immediately share your comment with not only hundreds of friends, but complete strangers throughout the world. Of course, if you consider this situation from the standpoint of a company, this is a scary proposition. Just as the aforementioned CEO "freaking out," so are marketers and public relations executives everywhere. For years, it's been the role of communications professionals to control public perception of their companies, and now any kid with a Twitter account or Facebook profile can ruin it all. That said, as a marketer, once you accept and embrace the fact that you cannot control the posting of negative comments about your company online, you can begin to formulate a plan for what you're going to do to respond to criticism. You could try to ignore it, of course. There are still plenty of companies that refuse to accept the fact that people are talking negatively about them. You could also try to delete things online. Sure, on your own Facebook page, you can delete whatever you want — and perhaps your company's lawyers could write letters to every Web publisher who ever allows negative comments to be published about you, demanding that those comments come down.

But the truth is, there's no way to entirely stop people from making negative posts about your company, whether you have an official Facebook page or not. So, why not prepare yourself and, instead of avoiding it, embrace negative feedback, comments, and criticism? Especially if you are dealing with this potential example. This idea might sound like a radical, damaging one — take a deep breath, and brace yourself.

THE DO-NOT-DELETE RULE

The do-not-delete (DND) rule states that unless a comment is obscene, profane, bigoted, or contains someone's personal and private information, never delete it from a social network. It might be best to illustrate the DND rule by first playing out a scenario in which you don't follow it. Control Freak Inc's Facebook Johnny Customer posts, "I just got a bill for $100 more than I was supposed to. You guys suck!" The frantic CEO insists deleting the comment from the page right away so nobody else sees it; it is promptly removed from the page. Johnny Customer logs on later that day to find his comment deleted. He is infuriated that the company has censored his complaint and reacts by starting a new Facebook group called "I Hate Control Freak Inc! Boycott Them!" He also makes a YouTube video singing about his hatred for the company, detailing his bad experience, and starts a Twitter trend with a hashtag: #controlfreakincsucks. As it turns out, Johnny Customer happens to be the captain of the football team at his school and a popular lead singer for band in town. Within twenty-four hours, thousands of people are posting negative comments on Control Freak Inc's wall, and worse yet, customers are canceling orders, and sales are down. Sure, this is a dramatic rendition of the situation and may not be the most likely occurrence. The point is, when you delete someone's comment, it is the ultimate "Screw you." It's like collecting someone's comment card, reading it in front of them, and then ripping it up in his or her face. You wouldn't do that, would you?

By responding quickly and publicly, you not only respond to someone's concern, but you also send the message out to the world at large that you're the kind of company that listens to its customers and fixes problems promptly. By taking the individual matter private, you avoid a public back-and-forth between company and customer, which wouldn't help anyone involved and prolongs the negative situation.

Refer to people by name, too, when you're apologizing: it goes a long way toward helping someone feel heard and understood. We're all human and we all make mistakes. Even the angriest of customers will recognize this truth and will be quick to forgive you, but only if you apologize and fix the problem as soon as possible.

Depending on the size of your organization, you'll need to make sure you have enough internal or external resources to handle complaints in a timely manner. You probably already have a sense of just how many complaints you typically receive, maybe from those traditional comment cards if you have them. Of course, comment cards used to get forwarded to a department, who read them, wrote back letters, and mailed the responses out a week later. In the online world, things happen a lot faster. Put on your consumer cap. If you had a complaint or question about something, how quickly would you want to be, or expect to be, answered? Of course you'd like to receive a response almost immediately, so you should answer your customers right away as well. As a rule of thumb, make sure you have the resources in place to answer people's negative comments within twenty-four hours or sooner, if possible. Even if the immediate response is, "I'm sorry. We'll look into that and get back to you with a private message within seventy-two hours," at least you're immediately telling the customer you care, and you're going to fix the problem as quickly as you can. After all, an angry customer is just like all of us: she wants to feel heard and understood. Sure, she may be more highly regulated than others, and sometimes, it's just not to enough to apologize.

For instance, as mentioned, feasible pharmaceutical companies often can't legally apologize for complaints made about their products. But the online feel of "We're sorry" can go a long way in helping make a customer feel heard and diffusing a potentially hazardous situation.

There are lots of ways to put an apology in writing without admitting any wrongdoing, too:

"I'm sorry you had this experience."

"We're sorry you feel this way."

"I'm so sorry you've had a problem."

"That sounds so frustrating. Sorry you felt like that."

Responding with a short but genuine apology is a great start but, equally important, you've got to be able to fix the problem. For many companies this means that the marketing and public relations departments have to work closely with the customer service team to resolve people's complaints in a timely manner. Remember, customers don't care what department you're in — they care if you can solve their problem or not. There's really no difference to customers between a public relations associate and a customer service rep.

FROM COMPLAINERS TO SUPPORTERS

Depending on how efficiently and effectively you can solve a customer's problem, you just might turn a hater into an admirer or even a major brand supporter. Consider if Johnny Customer, from our example, heard back from you immediately, and you were able to address his specific complaint with ease. His mind is likely to be changed about your company, and he might be so impressed and pleased that he recommends you to his peers. Consider the following real-life example of an unsatisfied Verizon customer.

FROM FOE TO FIOS TO FAN OF FIOS

Verizon FiOS is the television, Internet, and phone bundle offered by Fortune 500 company Verizon in select areas across the U.S.A. The Fans of FiOS Facebook page has been a marketing, promotions, and customer service asset for Verizon since 2008. When first launched, the page was designed to provide regional support for Verizon FiOS's marketing and promotions initiatives. Customers, however, are typically more concerned about their own service problems than about the marketing and promotional material posted — and they're not afraid to publicly state their issues. The FiOS team always attempts to quickly resolve such customer's issues in conjunction with Verizon policies and procedures.

Consider responding with surprise and delight. Responding with an apology and a quick solution to the problem is essential. But remember, unlike the comment card, which is a private matter, social media is of a public nature, so there's more at stake here when replying. Is there a way you can go above and beyond to fix the problem exceeding the unsatisfied customer's original expectations? Maybe you send a bonus gift in the mail, or refund the customer's invoice without telling her, or give her a deep discount on the next month's service. Consider the options, get creative, and the customer's next comment to all of her friends may be raving about the amazing company you are.

ACCEPT THAT COMPLAINTS ARE UNAVOIDABLE, REACT QUICKLY, AND YOUR CUSTOMER WILL ACCEPT YOU

No human is perfect, and therefore nor is any organization. Your company will surely make errors, and now, thanks to social networks, the whole world can easily find out about these mistakes. But you have the ability, also, to show the world how responsive a company you are. If you can respond quickly and authentically, with an apology and a solution, you can avoid damage to your reputation. Furthermore, if you provide an additional reward to your customers when the issue arises, you can actually turn your response and customer care into a marketing asset.

RESPOND TO GOOD COMMENTS

"Excuse me, sir," a well-dressed woman says to you in the aisle of your department store. "But I just wanted to take a moment to thank you for everything you and your company have done for me throughout the years. I am a long-time, happy customer and you've truly brought joy to my life. Thanks, and keep up the great work." You stare at her with a blank expression on your face, then turn and quickly walk away in fear there may be a complaining customer that you need to attend to elsewhere in the store. This situation is absurd, of course, and would never happen. You'd never reject a happy customer. Instead, you would welcome her with open arms and invite her to share more. You likely embrace your happiest customers — they remind you of what you're doing well and what your organization is all about. They're also the best unplanned part of your marketing agenda. Word-of-mouth endorsements and conversation from satisfied customers remains the most potentially powerful marketing tool you have. Yet each day, millions of positive comments to and about brands on social networks go unnoticed or are given no response.

Visit Facebook pages of most big organizations and you'll find people sharing stories, asking questions, and praising product's services almost always without a response. Do companies not have enough resources to address these posts? Are they too focused on maintaining a defensive posture in regards to the entire negative comments and therefore decide not to reply to comments at all? Do companies not see value in responding to positive posts? Whatever the reasons, they are making a mistake, possibly to your company's advantage. If your organization begins to foot only negative posts and comments, instead of positive ones and takes action in responding, you are ahead of the game. In fact, if other companies aren't doing a good job interacting with their customers or prospects through online social networking, your company looks even better to consumers when you take the initiative.

ACKNOWLEDGMENT ALONE GOES A LONG WAY — GET CREATIVE! Just as the two simple words "I'm sorry" go a long way when a customer complains, so do the words "Thank you" when a customer has something nice to say. "Thank you" says "You matter." "Thank you" says "We're listening." "Thank you" says "We appreciate you." It's best to further personalize your response as well, sharing your brand personality a little bit.

DEVELOP YOUR SOCIAL PERSONALITY

Brand personality is formed by giving your brand human traits when presenting your company to the public. Your brand's social personality sets you apart from other brands, giving your company unique features in an attempt to connect more directly and more humanly with your consumer. For example, the voice wording you use to respond to posts helps shape your personality. Here are several different ways to say thanks to a positive comment, while expressing the personality behind the brand.

Acknowledging your customer's positive feedback is easier today than it has ever been before. With the advent of the social access directly to your consumer, you are now able to show that, as a brand, you truly care about your customers. Responding in Your Brand's Voice Language is a major part of your brand identity.

Would a bank use the same language face-to-face with customers that a pizzeria would?

Would a pediatrician discuss a medical condition with her patients using the same language an oncologist would with his?

How about a major brand targeting its teenage customers using the same language as it does in an ad for adults?

Just as you use different language to talk to different customers face-to-face, or in advertising and marketing, based upon who they are and what your organization is all about, so must you consider the language you use on social networks in your responses.

CHILL ZONE SETS TONE

In fact, without having the advantage you have in face-to-face conversation, to inflect different emotions in your voice or use non-verbal communications, the tone of your written words on Facebook or Twitter is incredibly important. Think about the difference in perception when you read this, "Thank you very much for your feedback, sir. We appreciate your support." Compared to this, "Thanks, man. You rule!"

The truth is, people are more likely to buy products or services if they feel they know you and like you (both in general and in an online sense.) They are therefore much more apt to want to see something positive than something negative about your company. If you can authentically accelerate positive word-of-mouth about your organization, social media provides the tools for accomplishing this on a huge scale.

In the offline world, if a customer shares positive feedback, it's the perfect time to ask, "Do you have friends who would be appropriate for me to talk to?" Or, more passively, "Thanks. Please let your friends know on Facebook. Or when you receive a compliment, it's the perfect time to say, "Thanks. Please suggest this page to your friends! Click the link beneath our profile pic." The average person on Facebook has about 130 friends, but some people have as many as 5,000 (which is the maximum) and then many people following them. It is likely that your happy customer has more than a few friends who might also be interested in your page and will show their endorsements as well, creating a cycle of approval.

The situation is similar with Twitter. On Twitter, if you receive positive feedback, reply and ask the user to re-tweet, or share you with the user's followers. The average person on Twitter has 120 followers, and some have as many as 50,000 or more. Again, one recommendation on Twitter can go a long way toward building a new follower base.

None of this can happen however, if you don't recognize and thank your customers who actively follow and interact with each and every one of them.

Action Items:

1. Determine how you will allocate resources to respond to negative comments posted on social networks. Is it the visibility of the marketing department, the customer service department, or an agency?

2. Develop a plan to respond swiftly and publicly. Work with your lawyers to develop language that is okay by them and is as customer-friendly as possible.

3. Make sure you have enough resources to manage negative comments in a timely manner. Have the resources to not only respond to comments but actually fix the problems efficiently.
4. Write a list of five ways you can respond to negative situations positively, turn around customer complaints, and use "surprise and delight" to leverage otherwise negative situations.

ACTIVATE YOUR BRAND AMBASSADORS

Every small business knows that the handful of customers who are your die-hard people who swear by your service, all the time, or consistently refer others to your business. Big brands hopefully have even more of these people — folks I call: Brand Ambassadors.

Brand Ambassadors are those customers who love your organization no matter what. They are happy to tell others about your company without any special incentive, and without you even asking them to. Still, they'll be more likely to spread the word if you do ask, so why wouldn't you?

Picture Rod Tidwell telling Jerry Maguire (in the movie of the same name), "Jerry Maguire, my agent. You're my ambassador of quan." Tidwell describes "quan" as "the entire package" made up of love, respect, community, and the dollars, too. Come the end of the day, this quality, "quan," is what all companies are searching for: a community built of mutual respect resulting in financial growth for the business and satisfied, loyal customers. Brand Ambassadors, or so-called "ambassadors of quan," want to share the "special sauce" that you've got — all you have to do is tell them to. It helps that now, thanks to social networks and privacy settings, you can quickly tell how many online friends people have. Online influence varies greatly from one person to the next, and since all organizations have limited resources, you'll want to find Brand Ambassadors who not only adore you but also have lots of friends, fans, or followers.

Once you've identified your Brand Ambassadors, you can do much more than just thank them for being customers. You can reward them with incentives, special perks, and exclusive content. For example, provide them with online tools or samples of your product so they can share with friends or hand the products out at parties they might host with your help. You can give them multimedia content such as pictures and videos and encourage them to create "mashups," adding their own voice and interpretation to your material before passing it along to followers.

The goal is to activate your customers who love you enough to regularly share their passion for you publicly.

FULL DISCLOSURE

You'll want to amplify your brand ambassadors' voices as much as possible — just make sure you have them disclose their relationship with you. If you end up giving them anything of material value, the Federal Trade Commission requires that reviewers disclose they received something in exchange for posting a review or other comments. For instance, you can't give someone a trip to your resort in exchange for them blogging or writing on Facebook about their experience, unless they clearly disclose that they received a free trip in exchange for the review. (More on transparency in the Building Trust chapter).

Word-of-mouth marketing has always been a good business practice, but today, the ability to effectively and efficiently utilize it through social networks is unparalleled.

In the past, if a celebrity visited your store, you'd certainly treat him exceptionally well and ask him to spread the word about his experience. Now it is important to think of every customer as an online celebrity with followers, friends, and, above all, influence. Sure, not everyone who posts on your Facebook wall or tweets about you has as much sway or trendsetting ability as some "celebrities," but they certainly can spread the word on your behalf easily and quickly — especially if you thank and encourage them. Some users probably have more online influence than so-called celebrities, too!

Action Items:
1. Create a social brand bible for response. Determine what your brand's voice should be like in its responses to customers on social networks. Fun? Serious? Personal? Professional? Write down several different specific ways, based on this brand voice that you would say "Thank you" to a happy customer.
2. Determine the necessary resources to respond to every customer with a comment or question who posts on a social network, based on your understanding of the current number of customers, fans,

and followers your organization has. How will your staff do this? Will you do it internally or use an outside vendor? What about nights and weekends?

3. Determine formal or informal ways you can reward your most loyal and influential customers in order to accelerate the positive word-of-mouth recommendations they have. What assets can you offer? What expectations will you have? How can you be assured that they are following the laws of the land and disclosing to their friends what they received from you?

TRULY VALUING ALL YOUR CUSTOMERS

Every company says it cares about its customers, but so many don't actually back up this claim on social networks, let alone elsewhere. You wouldn't hang up the phone on a customer or walk away from one face-to-face, so don't ignore them on Facebook, Twitter, or any other online social networking medium either. By valuing each customer, at least enough to say "Thanks," you show the world that you are truly an organization that cares about its customers. By throwing in some surprise delight and getting your biggest fans to further spread the word your "quan" can travel a long way.

Let's take this customer care example, "Thank you for calling us. This is your customer care advocate, how can I be of service to you today?" You hear this on the opposite end of the line. "Great", you think, this sounds like someone who can help. "I'd like to dispute part of my bill that I don't understand," you reply. "Account number, please," the customer care advocate responds. Though you entered that number into your phone keypad just moments ago when you first called, you proceed to give the representative the information anyhow. "I'm sorry," the customer care advocate replies. "There's nothing I can do about that problem. You'll have to speak with the billing department, and they're only open Monday through Friday. Can I help you with anything else today?" The employee is just doing his job, of course, but all his job entails is following a script. Not only does this interaction leave you frustrated at the company's inability to help you with your problem, but it also may leave you scratching your head about the inauthenticity of considering a phone agent a "customer care advocate." In no way does this employee's job seem to involve caring or advocating for you, the customer.

How about "financial counselors"? Have you ever received assistance from a "financial counselor" who in fact is an insurance salesperson concerned little, if at all, with helping you sort out your financial issues? Not everybody with the job title of customer care advocate or financial counselor is inauthentic. There are likely lots of great folks doing those jobs. But the job titles themselves are misleading, intentionally or not. Of course, this inauthenticity does not apply only to job titles: brand promises from slogans, advertisements, and websites are often guilty of the same inaccuracies or false representations.

Many large companies have a hard time being authentic in their interactions with customers. As organizations get larger, it becomes difficult to manage higher volumes of staff and clients. To deal with this growth, managers develop models and processes, and customer service centers create scripts. These attempts at efficiency might cause some aspects of the organization to run smoothly, but in dealing with customers, they make it easy to miss the mark. Models, processes, and scripts will not help you connect with your consumer. Instead, such impersonal devices create a division between your service or product and customer, with a loss of valuable human interaction.

Social media provides an opportunity to reverse this trend for larger organizations and to showcase authenticity for smaller ones. Your company can actually "be human" in dealing with its customers through current social networks. You'll find that your customers will respond positively and appreciate you more as well. Be warned, the opposite of this is true as well if you try to deal with huge numbers of customers on social networks in an inauthentic, highly processed way, it can and will backfire. Before going any further, I should point out specifically what I mean when I say that you have to be authentic on social networks. Overall, you have to be human and demonstrate a personality. No one wants to feel as if she is talking to a machine or dealing with someone who cannot empathize with her situation.

The online social Web is all about human interaction connecting with one another on some level. As a company, you need to want to connect with your consumers or prospects in a personal or individual manner. You also have to be flexible and responsive, with the ability to cater to a customer's various or changing needs, wants, opinions, and ideas. Become part of the online conversation and truly seek to understand your consumers and the role your product or service plays, or could play, in their actual life. While in the context of representing your brand, you, and anyone else connected with your organization, have to be the person you really are — you can't fake it anymore when it comes to dealing with the consumer.

Aaron Sorkin, who wrote the screenplay for the hit movie *The Social Network*, about the founding of Facebook and its early days, told Stephen Colbert in a television interview (aired September 30, 2010) that social networking is more of a performance than a reality. He so glaringly missed the point. On the contrary, social networking, done well, is authentic and real, unlike Sorkin's scripts.

Others have speculated that social network users are narcissists, sharing their every move with the world (think when users post what kind of cereal they had for breakfast this morning). Yes, there are some people, and companies, who use social networks for such self-centered purposes and fail to see the true possibilities of harnessing the online social Web. Such users are short-sighted and in many ways tragic, as the promise of social network communication holds much greater potential.

Facebook, for example, can in fact be a place for people to authentically connect with one another and for companies to build true and long-lasting relationships with customers and prospects.

BE AN IMPROV SHOW, NOT A MUSICAL

Musicals, plays, and operas are all wonderful, traditional forms of entertainment. Theatergoers attend, sit back, and relax, and the performers "put on a show." Performances can be subtle and nuanced but are often loud, larger-than-life productions, especially musicals. Most musicals include lots of color and sound expensive. They use scenery, props, and costumes in an attempt to "wow" the audience and leave a lasting impression. The same script is performed night after night, and with stellar writing, acting, singing, and directing, the show comes together and wins over the crowd.

Improvisation comedy shows, on the other hand, usually have little to no set and almost nothing scripted. Improv features several performers, who interact with the audience throughout each show by soliciting ideas for skits then basing their performances on audience suggestions each night. Unlike a musical, every show is different, but as long as the audience brings creative or interesting ideas and high energy, and the performers are talented, it makes for an incredible experience.

Your brand, company, or organization can create such an experience for your customers and prospects on networks. Even better news is that this can be done without the huge budget of a Broadway show or a television commercial. It will, however, require a fundamental shift in the way you see media and marketing, now that social media has enabled a two-way conversation between the company and the consumer. You'll have to think less about "putting on a show" and more about building an excellent team that is flexible, able to go with the flow, responsive, and engaged. And unlike in improv, in which performers are playing different parts every night, your team needs to rely on its own authenticity as unique, individual people.

DEVELOP AN AUTHENTIC VOICE

Advertising has traditionally been more like a Broadway musical than an improv show. The goal has been to create a brilliant distraction to get people's attention, be noticeable, or generate buzz, even if the products or services offered often lack a sense of authenticity. Consumers, however, have gotten used to talking to each other through social networks with a level of humanity they have come to expect from all users.

Now, as an advertiser or company, you need to join in this conversation, and when you do so, your organization must keep your consumers' expectations in mind. You have to be an authentic human being in your interactions. Anything less and your consumer might consider the conversation nothing more than a marketing ploy, no better than if you repeated a bland corporate mantra. Consider what your brand or organization is really like. How can you convert our mission statement or the "About Us" page on your website into actual conversations you'll facilitate and be involved in each day on Facebook and Twitter? You need to let the world know about your company's, or brand's, personality while showing that you truly care about your consumers and are willing to put the time in to make a connection with them.

REGULATING DISCUSSIONS

Hopefully, your organization already has protocols for how customer service reps interact with customers, how salespeople pitch prospects, or how public relations executives talk to traditional media reps. With the advent of social networking, all of that "talk" online is a matter of public record forever. There is a tendency, especially in large organizations, to carefully regulate that speech, making sure it meets corporate and legal guidelines and that nobody says the "wrong thing."

For example, corporate communications and legal departments may be concerned about their employees or representatives going "off message", making negative comments, or admitting liability through an apology. That attitude is a mistake on social networks and renders authentic communication nearly impossible. The more you try to regulate brand conversations, the more impersonal you'll make them, and the less customers will respond. Worse still, the less flexible and authentic you are, the more it will show, and the less you'll be trusted.

Remember, online, your trust and reputation with customers is everything "happy" at your company. So what can you do to keep the lawyers but maintain that all-important authenticity? The best solution is to develop a set of guidelines for what tone of voice will be used and what you really can't say. Then, make sure that trustworthy people are representing the organization on social media platforms.

THE AUTHENTIC CELEBRITY

Social media provides a platform for celebrities, who typically have had to hire marketers or publicists to promote them and speak directly with consumers and fans. Actors, musicians, athletes, politicians, authors, and other public figures all have excellent opportunities to grow their fan bases, shape public perception, and accomplish their objectives by harnessing online social networking. Authenticity must be a key part of their plan, though. Ideally, any public persona is Facebooking and tweeting for themselves, an authenticity that is impossible to top. Keep in mind that mobile phones allow anyone to share information on the run, opening a world of instant communication no matter where you are or what you are doing. Of course there will be times when fan interaction may not be feasible, and it certainly is not possible for public figures to respond to each and every comment from admirers on their own. Agencies or staffers are commonly hired to help in this process, but still attempt to make the response as personal as possible, sometimes indicating when they, and not the celebrity, are responding by sharing the initials of their name. Being up front as to who is actually responding on behalf of the public figure maintains authenticity.

Action Items:
1. If you're a one-person operation or a very small business, write down five things you could say that would seem authentic or that sound like marketing-speak to a customer. Then write five examples of how you could say the same messages in a more authentic way on Facebook.
2. If you are part of a large organization, create a plan for how to represent yourself authentically. Recognize that authenticity won't be easy but that it's essential. Meet with key stakeholders and management at your organization to determine how you can make communication more authentic across all channels, especially on social networks.
3. If you already have a social media policy, examine it carefully to ensure that it encourages authentic communication, and tweak it if it doesn't. If you don't yet have a social media policy, draft one now.
4. If multiple people are responding on Twitter on behalf of your organization, have them sign tweets with their name or initials.

BUILDING TRUST: TRANSPARENCY IS NO LONGER NEGOTIABLE

Traditional marketers have worked for years at shaping people's opinions about brands and organizations using advertising and other linear marketing tactics. Marketers may be tempted to stretch the truth on social networks in order to achieve similar objectives, I can't stress this point any stronger: You must be as honest and transparent as possible when using social media. Honesty and transparency build a direct relationship between you and the customer, and any deviation from these values can erode brand trust forever. In an age when it's virtually impossible to hide the truth, don't bother trying. If you're not ready to face the facts about your products or organization and share them with consumers, don't join the conversation yet. Once you're committed to creating a presence in social media outlets, there's no going back, and you really have no choice but to embrace transparency. If it seems intuitive to you to be honest, that's terrific. But too many marketers have employed dishonest tactics in trying to reach the consumer, losing sight of the simple importance of telling the truth. With the advent of social media, consumers expect transparency from companies and organizations more than ever before.

JUST LIKE DATING: THE MORE OPEN YOU ARE, THE BETTER

Anyone who has ever dated knows that openness and honesty factors in establishing a relationship. When one person has trouble opening up to the other, the potential relationship is threatened — wouldn't you think someone had something to hide if they were not completely candid with you? The same situation applies to your company: if you have nothing to hide, only positive outcomes will result from increased transparency.

If a date completely opened up to you the first time you went out and shared her innermost secrets in the spirit of transparency, however, it would probably be uncomfortable and similarly, as a company, just because you're supposed to be transparent doesn't mean you have to share trade secrets, profit margins, or insider information with all of your customers. A lot of that information would be off-putting, even to the most curious customer.

In general, though, when you share insights into your company's values and culture and encourage an honest discussion of the decisions you've made, customers will trust feeling closer to you and want to strengthen their relationships with you. Just like in dating. Being transparent doesn't mean you have to share everything about your organization, but the more honest insight you provide, the better.

Ask a lot of questions! People responsible for social media at organizations often lament, "Nobody's responding to our posts on Facebook and Twitter." Especially if you don't have a large organization with many thousands of fans, receiving responses to, or comments on, your content can be challenging. To combat this issue, start with the basics. Consider whether you would be more likely to respond to a question or a statement in a conversation.

WHAT IS THE MARKETING VALUE OF QUESTIONS?

Put on your consumer caps and think about what companies say to you across marketing channels and how it makes you feel. Advertisers have always sought to make an emotional connection with their customers. Consider what better builds an emotional connection: when advertisers tell you about their companies or when they ask you your opinions about them?

Asking questions creates marketing value in these four ways:

1. Helping you guide the social media conversation without appearing forceful
2. Allowing you to become consumer-centric marketers rather than brand-centered marketers
3. Demonstrating that you value openness, honesty, and feedback (three values customers and prospects universally hold in high regard)
4. Showing that you care about what your customers have to say

Questions build an emotional connection between you and the consumer, and they generate conversations about your customers' pain points, problems, and needs. As customers have discussions with each other, and with you, you'll gain mindshare, increasing the likelihood that they'll turn to you for your products and services when needed.

WHAT IS THE INSIGHT VALUE OF QUESTIONS?

Questions on social networks lead to conversations that clearly have marketing value. But even if they didn't have such value, the insight you can glean alone from them is immense. Companies' research and development departments, commonly known as R&D, routinely spend many thousands or even millions of dollars on programs, such as focus groups, surveys, and customer marketing research, to gain insight into their customers or prospects. Yet, once you've built up a following on Facebook, Twitter or both, you can tap into these communities on a regular basis without spending a dime! These online networks are living proof!

There are such things as living, breathing focus groups. You can ask your community questions about attitudes, their opinions, their knowledge of competitors, and an infinite number of other topics.

Try asking simple questions such as the following to start:

"What can we do better?"

"What was your best and worst experience with us?"

"What do you think of our recent advertisement?"

Eventually you can also cut or limit the traditional focus group and research activity you do offline, saving money and providing you with a direct, real-time audience whose responses to your questions are almost instant.

In an age of growing transparency, asking questions publicly to gather insight is best. But what if you want to gather insights privately? Even in that case, you can create a private survey online and then solicit people to participate through your social communities. And when you solicit people, in order to generate a better response rate, ask a question! "Who'd like to participate in a survey about us?" will yield a response more often than "Click better here to participate in a survey about us" every time. Remember, asking questions has a natural tendency to elicit answers.

Action Items:

1. Write down a list of the topics of conversation your customers typically talk about. Remember, when you brainstorm, write about topics that have something to do with your brand or organization, and also some that have nothing to do with your brand. What do your customers like to talk about? What can they have a spirited discussion about?

2. Based upon the topics your customers discuss, write a list of questions you could ask them publicly on Facebook or Twitter to stimulate interesting discussion.

3. What questions could you ask your fans to glean insight into what they want from you and how you could do a better job serving your customers? If your organization has done market research, surveying, or focus group testing in the past, consider how you might translate some of that work to a social media landscape.

4. Do you have any projects that might be well served by crowd sourcing? Determine whether you have any upcoming design updates, new products or packaging, or other opportunities you could ask your customers and fans to help you with publicly.

GETTING YOUR MESSAGE OUT THERE, CONSISTENTLY!

Creating and sharing valuable content will provide you with a great reputation and return but only over time and through consistent effort and commitment.

Articles are no longer solely written and shared by professional services firms. Now every company and brand can post articles they have written in-house or found to their blogs and Facebook pages. They can tweet and re-tweet valuable information throughout their entire community simultaneously. You are essentially able to publish any amount of valuable information with the click of a button that has the potential to be seen by millions of users.

Venture capitalist Fred Wilson and many others have said that links are the economy of the social Web. Once you are connected through such links, your audience grows exponentially.

Writing and sharing great articles can provide your community with valuable information, no matter what you're responsible for marketing. If it's a food product or restaurant, you can share great recipes. If you're marketing a clothing brand, you can share articles about the latest fashions. If it's a hotel or airline, you can share articles about travel tips.

The most important thing is to think about your target audience and provide articles they will find valuable. What would you find useful if you were on the receiving end of a status update? What would you like to see from your company? Keep in mind, no matter what your organization sells, you're not selling that here. Instead, you're selling your expertise. You're selling your reputation. You're selling your credibility. And, of course; you're not actually trading this content directly for something in return: you're giving it away. But is it worth it to a thought leader in whatever space you're in? Is it worth it if in the future you never have to sell anything because people consider you the top expert in your niche, and they come to you to buy your product or service before searching elsewhere?

For consumer brands, you might want to create a fun game to play, a comic that makes people laugh, or a free mobile or Facebook application, all of which can provide entertainment and practical value. Be warned, however, that the cost of developing your own online game or application can be huge and therefore is riskier than writing a quick article.

Another way to provide valuable content is through videos. You may find it easier to create 60-120 second long videos talking about how to do things yourself, top-five tips, or any other content you might have traditionally written in an online post or article. For many, filming videos is easier than writing, and videos also have the added benefit of better showcasing your organization's personality than the written word might be able to.

Here are a few quick guidelines for creating video content:

1. Use a flip cam. There's usually no reason to waste money on more expensive equipment.
2. Keep it short and sweet. People's attention spans online are short — no longer than two minutes.
3. Share the videos everywhere. Share on YouTube and Facebook and consider using a service such as Tube Mogul which allows you to share your videos on dozens of different platforms.
4. Have fun with it. This shows in your final product. (It also shows if the person on camera is uncomfortable or anxious).

No matter what medium you decide to use, content and value can be as simple or complex as you want. The main criterion however, is that you deliver something useful to your customers or communities and truly ask for nothing in return.

Action Items:
1. Brainstorm and write down all the ways in which you can provide value to your target audience without focusing on marketing yourself or selling your company to them at all. What will help your customers get the most information, entertainment, functionality, or a combination of these?
2. Write down the format or formats your organization is most capable of using to provide your audience with valuable content on the Internet. Will it be through blog articles you write, videos you create, or a game or application? Or will you comb the Web looking for interesting and useful content based around a particular set of topics and share your findings?

3. Create several pieces of content in which you think your customers would find valuable. Before you share the content on Facebook or another social network, share it with a friend or two to test it. Do they find it worthwhile? Equally important, do they see it as an advertisement for your organization?

4. Determine whether your organization may be a fit for Groupon-like model of deeply discounting a product or service, with a guarantee of increased sales through group offers. It's not for everyone but can be a way to provide value to customers while insuring a profitable return for your company.

STORIES BRING YOUR COMPANY TO LIFE

When you hear the story of how a company was born or one about the impact an organization has had on a customer's life or about the unique experience of a group's staff member or partner, you feel an emotional connection with that company. Social media, especially blogs and online video, allows you to share your stories with your customers, prospects, and the world, further building powerful connections. In the past, storytelling to the masses was expensive and could only be accomplished through television advertising or a public relations executive pitching a major newspaper. Now, storytelling is free, or near-free, through social media. Said attorney, entrepreneur, and blogger Matt Weiss, "People love hearing stories. It goes back to primitive tribal times when we used to sit around the campfire."

With social media, consumers are in full control the whole time. If you're not captivating, you can lose them at any time. I use storytelling as a vehicle to get people to pay attention and then keep paying attention. Your company has at least one story to tell.

Ask the following questions to generate some ideas:

How did your company get started?

How did you survive the toughest of times?

Who are some of the key customers you've had?

What kinds of funny or interesting things have happened to customers or staff over the years?

Has your company or its staff had some moments in the past which would now make incredible stories?

What charitable organizations does your company support?

Stories humanize brands and make them talk-able, both online and offline. Stories can be told with text but are often best told through pictures and videos. They can be told by customers, employees, or management — they just need to be authentic.

HOW YOU STARTED

No matter how large your company is today, when it started, it was just your founder or founders with a dream and a plan. Every organization has humble beginnings, and by reminding people of this, you connect with your customers and keep them from considering your group as faceless, a giant or too corporate. You can spend millions of advertising dollars to buy television commercials to tell the story of how you got started or produce gorgeous full-color brochures and mail them out to the world. Or you can tell this story online, using your website, blog, or any social channels, for little to no cost.

BUILD WORD OF MOUTH INTO YOUR PRODUCTS AND SERVICES

The most effective way of inspiring your customers to tell others about you is to have buzz-worthy, talk-able products and services in the first place. These products or features are the types that truly make you go, "Wow!" as a customer or, in their very nature, create passionate users. Take Facebook itself, for instance. It has grown from several hundred users to several hundred million users in just five years, not because of any clever marketing whatsoever but simply because it has built amazing products that people love and continue to spread the word about it.

SOCIAL MEDIA IS NOT JUST MARKETING

Social media leveraging is not just marketing or public relations. There is no way to successfully use social media as an organization if you simply silo it to marketing or advertising. In order to optimize the results from your social media use, you have to integrate understanding and practice across a diverse group of functions and departments in your organization. Of course, social media provides outlets for marketing, public relations, and advertising, but it also involves customer service, customer relationship management, sales, operations, human resources, and research and development.

If you have a very small operation, you're used to handling many tasks on your own. But assuming you're part of a larger organization, let's review various departments and consider how each one might integrate and encourage social media in order to optimize the customer experience at every corner.

Advertising. Include social media links and value propositions to customers in all paid linear media. For example, television, radio, print, e-mail, websites, and direct mail should all include social media links, text-to-connect opportunities, or both. The advertising may also handle social network ads themselves, a growing part of most budgets.

Marketing. Determine, create, execute, and measure promotions, contests, giveaways, and other marketing programs and content to be run on Facebook and other social networks. Marketing is where social media typically lives right now, even though it should have a home in each department.

Public relations. Listen to customer comments on works and blogs and respond in a swift manner. The social network's most influential bloggers and other key customers reach out to them to pitch them on participating in programs and customer service. Listen to customer complaints and reach across social networks and respond. Encourage customers to reach out via traditional channels to share on their feedback publicly on social networks.

Operations. Create and implement social media policy. Ensure that all staff are fluent in understanding company social media links and practices and that signage, receipts, and any other customer touch points include opportunities to interact and share.

Sales. Listen carefully to prospects online as well as major potential partners and distributors. Leverage listening to create best- value propositions. Use LinkedIn and individual Facebook profiles to meet and engage prospects.

Take note, customers don't care what department you're working in. When should a customer's comment on Facebook be answered by customer service versus sales, versus public relations, versus marketing, versus your agency? That's all up to you. The truth is, the key challenge isn't making sure you know exactly who should answer what kind of comment and when. Instead, the issue is making sure that as many people as possible are fluent in social media, are part of the team, and are treating every customer well!

Customers don't care about your job title or what department you're working in. If they have problems, then they want solutions. When you're looking for something specific in a supermarket and you find a staff person and ask for help, a good supermarket will have that staff person trained to walk you to the correct aisle. The employee will help you, with a smile, whether he or she happens to be the butcher, the baker, a cashier, or a janitor. The situation applies to the use of social media, too. Try thinking of every post on Facebook, Twitter, or your blog as one that could have been written by the most important celebrity customer you've ever had, and you'll be more likely to treat every customer and every post with great care, no matter your official department or role.

Ensure that the website is as integrated with social media as possible. If you have only a tiny link at the bottom of your website, "Like us on Facebook and follow us on Twitter," you're not leveraging the opportunity to connect to people. Facebook's social plug-ins, including the Like button and other assorted interactive elements such as "Share" and "Recommend," are imperative to smoothly and deeply integrating Facebook into your Web presence.

Imagine if, for instance, instead of trying to sell people your product or service, whatever it may be, on your website, all you did was try to convince people to like your website's content. As discussed previously, you'd get fewer sales at first, of course, but over time, more and more visitors to your website would see how many people liked you. More importantly, you'd increase the likelihood that one of the site's next visitors sees that her friend has already given your site, services, products, or content personal approval. Are there any sales or promotional content anywhere on the Web more valuable than the honest words, "Your friend likes this?"

WE LIVE IN A WORLD OF INSTANT GRATIFICATION

New technologies have made it easier than ever for consumers to access what they want. People don't need to go to bookstores to get books, flower stores to get flowers, or shoe stores to get shoes. People also don't need to buy newspapers or magazines to read articles. Thanks to the growth of mobile food trucks, you don't even need to go to restaurants to buy meals anymore in many cities. Now is the best time ever to be a consumer. Just remember, as a marketer, it is necessary that you make it as easy and efficient as possible for people to access your products, services, or content. How can you bring it to them, wherever they are on the Web? Where in the marketing and communications process can you remind people to engage with you on the social Web?

Action Items
1. Determine who else besides you at your organization can have a role in using social media to interact with customers. Form a cross-departmental task force to better integrate social media into all of your business practices and operations.
2. Closely examine all your available inventory, assets, time, and space you have to promote your Facebook presence. As you grow your Facebook presence, where can you remind people to join the conversation? Where can you share your value proposition for "liking" your company and following you? Have you integrated social media links into your traditional advertising packaging, and website yet?
3. Integrate Facebook's Like button into as many products and objects on your website as make sense. The easier you make it to be "likeable," the more likeable you'll become.

SPEAKING TO LEVERAGE YOUR RESULTS

One of the most efficient way to grow your brand and to accelerate the results you are getting in your business, is to speak. This includes both online and offline speaking, but right now, lets focus purely on the offline method.

You have a few options when it comes to speaking but the first thing you must do is actively make a decision that you want to speak. You must then decide whether you want to promote and run your own events to speak at, or find other people's events to speak at, or both! There are benefits and challenges with both.

When you are running and speaking at your own event, obviously there is a lot more work involved. You and your team will need to market and promote the event, fill the event, cover all the expenses but ultimately, if you are selling at the event, you keep one hundred percent of any income that is created after covering your expenses.

If you are more interested in speaking at other people's events, you often simply need to turn up and speak. The organiser of the event will cover all of the expenses and promotion responsibilities. If it is someone else's event however, you have to play by their rules. Including time frame, potential speaker fee, you may not be allowed to self-promote or sell your product, etc. Even if you are not allowed to sell your product from someone else's stage, it is still great exposure, and if your brand is positioned well online, people will be able to search your name, find your website and landing pages and eventually filter through your systems to convert into clients.

At the end of the day, the more you can speak and get yourself out in front of people, the more that this is going to increase your visibility. The best thing is, it is a leveraged model. If you can speak for an hour to 200 people for example, that is much more efficient than speaking to 200 people individually for an hour each...

If you are just starting out and you have never spoken before, there are a few things you should focus on:

1. Find speaking engagements. Network. Grow your audience. Connect with people and offer to speak for free and add value.

2. Don't trick yourself into thinking that you need professional speaker training in order to be brilliant. Of course, any training that you do undertake is going to accelerate your results and your impact, however, some of the best, most influential speakers have had zero, or very little, physical speaker training and they simply show up authentically as them and are focused on sharing their message.

3. Focus on giving first. Give, give, give. The more you can give to the audience the more likely you are to generate leads and grow your following. Where possible, always give something away for free in exchange for their email address, so that you can continue to market to them and add value in the future.

ONLINE LEVERAGED SPEAKING

We touched on the traditional offline speaking strategies, but in this day and age, you absolutely have to be speaking online in order to accelerate your results in a leveraged way. A great way to do just this is by running online webinars, free teleconferences, Zoom Meetings, Google Hangouts, Periscopes, Facebook Mentions Live as well as many other platforms.

The process when it comes to online leveraged speaking is simple. The purpose of speaking online is the same as speaking offline: increasing visibility, building a following, reaching many people at one time and ultimately offering your audience your product or service. Many people are drawn to the online leveraged speaking models due to the amount of ease associated with it.

Proving you and your audience have an internet connection, you can run the online event from wherever you please in the world, and people can tune in from everywhere in the world, unlike having to turn up at a specific place for an offline event.

Here are the key points to follow and consider when running online leveraged speaking events:

1. Promote the online event to your audience
2. Provide roughly forty-five minutes of content and then fifteen minutes of presenting your product or your service
3. Ensure you record your live event so you can turn it into a product or use it as a sales tool over and over again in the future.

Ultimately, to accelerate the results of your brand, you want to combine both online and offline leveraged speaking strategies to ensure that you are reaching as many people as possible, in as many powerful ways as possible.

PRICE POINT INCREASES

Once your brand is getting great results through your product and service launches, you will want to consider increasing your price points as one way to accelerate your results. The amount that you are charging for your products and services are directly proportional to what you believe they are worth, and, in a personal brand like this, they are directly proportional to what YOU believe YOU are worth. As you start seeing people join your tribe and get great results, often your own self-belief and self-worth increases so, naturally, you should look at increasing your prices when you understand the amount of value that you are giving to people.

Often people battle with the thought of increasing their prices, as their scarcity mindset sets in, "What if it's overpriced and no one buys it any more?" When and if that mindset starts to happen, you need to catch it and recognize it as scarcity and choose to think differently.

At the end of the day, if someone is investing $47 a month for your product, chances are, they would be willing to invest $57 a month. If someone is investing $3997 for your product, chances are, they would be willing to invest $4997 for the same amount of value.

When increasing your price points, you always want to ensure you look after your current tribe members as these are your loyal clients who stepped up and invested first. It's not recommended to increase the price points for your current tribe members, but instead, increase the price points for new clients.

A great way to do this, is to let your audience know that your prices will be increasing. You can run a special offer of accessing the current price for a certain amount of days, before it goes up to the new price. This encourages people to take action and moves all the people forward who have been sitting on the fence and watching you. It also makes your current clients feel great when they can see the prices increase and they know they have been looked after as it hasn't increased for them.

YOU CAN'T DO THIS ALL ON YOUR OWN

If your head is feeling overloaded at this point, then that is perfect! As most likely you've realised, that you really can't do all of this on your own! And please, don't try and do all of this on your own. Last time I checked, you were looking to build an incredible, global brand that is going to make a massive impact in the world and that can't be done with just one person.

Take Richard Branson, Oprah Winfrey and Tony Robbins to name a few. These are people who are extremely well-known, have incredible brands and are making a massive impact in this world, yet, they have one thing in common that is the most important thing to take note of right now: They don't try and do it all themselves. They understand that they are only as powerful as the team that they have around them.

People often ask, how do I know when I should be hiring and expanding my team? What tasks should I start getting them to do? And the answers are simple: You should start as soon as possible. Remember, the goal is to have you completely replaced from the day-to-day running of your business by the twelve-month mark. If you can do this earlier then, bravo! And when it comes to what you should start getting your new team members to do, again it is simple: Anything you either aren't good at or don't enjoy doing, you should be outsourcing and getting your team to do for you.

KEYS TO HIRING A SUCCESSFUL TEAM

Everyone has a different belief system, different values, different dreams, desires, fears, weaknesses, strengths — the list goes on. When you dive deep into understanding human behavior, you really get a grasp of just how unique and complex humans really are. And connecting with someone becomes an art form, and a confusing one at that, once you really start to delve into the complexities. And connecting with MORE than one person? With all of those different factors that make people tick? NOW we're in a super challenging place!

I get asked all the time, "How do you empower a big team? How do you keep everyone motivated and on track?" And before we get into that, it's important to realize you really are only as powerful as your team. If you don't know how to lead, inspire and communicate with your team, it will be a challenge to get big results rapidly.

I see so many people trying to get results managing or leading a team of people, and when they find their team is no longer engaged or following them, they feel bewildered as they're not sure what steps to take. If you have been in that place, you'll know what I mean. And if you haven't, and you're growing a business, it's coming, so listen closely.

It's a BIG topic when it comes to leading a powerful team, in fact, I could create an entire online product about it, but if I were to give you the ONE THING to focus on, it would be vision. Leaders have the ability to speak belief into a vision for people that they are not yet able to see in their mind.

And if you're asking 'how?' We can break vision down further into three key sections:

- Your vision
- The team vision
- Individual vision

Firstly, as a leader, you must be super clear on your own vision, what you want and where you are headed. If you're not, this whole game falls apart!

Once your own vision is rock solid and charged with intensely positive emotion, turn your focus to the team vision. What is the vision for the team, where is the team headed and what are they looking to achieve? Once that is solidified, it is your job to enroll each and every team member into the vision of the team. At the end of the day, people want to be loved, appreciated and most importantly, they want to belong.

So many people don't have a team or tribe that has a clear vision and they are looking and waiting for a leader to step up and enroll them into a strong team vision that they can be a part of. Think about this for a second — have you actively worked or trained your leaders to work individually to enroll every single person in your team to be a part of your team's culture and vision?

Then last but certainly not least, people need an individual vision. This is the most important thing when it comes to leading a powerful team, as if people don't understand what's in it for them, in the long term, they will leave your team, even if the team vision is strong. People need to know that they are moving forward to their own personal dreams and desires by being aligned with the vision. At the end of the day, if they do not have a leader helping them build a strong and distinct vision, you will find that people won't stand beside you forever.

When you focus on these key elements of vision you'll find that people will do their best work, will stay fully engaged and will LOVE being a part of your team.

DEVELOPING JOINT VENTURES TO ACCELERATE RESULTS

A mentor of mine once said to me, "There is no competition in business, there is only collaboration. And collaboration equals growth and profit." The minute that you have developed and launched your brand, you need to start looking for people who you can partner with and market with. Being partnered with other credible and influential people makes you, your business and your credibility even stronger.

When considering who to partner with and market with you should be considering:

1. The person's values. Are they in alignment with yours? Do you like what they stand for? Do you like the way they do business? Association with another brand can either dramatically accelerate or dramatically kill your business, so be careful here!
2. The person's outcomes. What are they looking to achieve? Why do they want this? What is driving them? Is it the same things that drive you to your success?
3. Their overall big goals with this partnership. Where do they see the relationship heading? What do they want from it long term? Why? What will it give them vs what will it give you?

Once you have found people who are on your wave length and that have the same values as you, you always want to make sure that any partnerships or launches that you do together are a win-win for both parties. It's recommended that you take the partnership one launch at a time and, if it feels right, you'll promote it, and vice versa. So it's done on "feeling" rather than promoting by obligation. When you promote by obligation, it can throw you completely out of alignment and your audience will feel this too, and, chances are, it will not be a successful launch.

Ultimately, if you can create a group of eight to twelve people who are totally in alignment with your vision and your mission of your brand, you'll want to team up and work together to really accelerate each others launches and successes. No one in business makes it alone, and if you have goals to go to eight figures and beyond in your brand, then this group launch strategy will be one of the most powerful things you can do to accelerate your brand and your results.

SUMMARY

$\mathcal{E}$veryone has a powerful personal brand locked away inside them. Everyone has a message that they are called to share with the world. And when you align what's on the inside with action that you take on the outside, magical things can happen, fast.

The strategies are simple in their execution, as long as you are super clear on your message to the world and the kind of people you want to attract.

You have the system, you have the steps and now it is up to you to implement it. Of course, your speed of implementation will depend on the action you take and also if you have a coach beside you accelerating everything for you.

If this book has shown you that you are ready to step up and take further action in developing, launching and accelerating your personal brand, make sure you apply through www.reganhillyer.com to see if you are eligible to participate in one of the live, in-person, or online Be Your Brand Masterminds. These programs are not for everyone, but after a short chat with the team at Regan Hillyer International, they'll know whether you're the right person to be a part of the Masterminds.

Go out there, share your true message with the world, make an incredible impact and remember, you absolutely CAN have it ALL!

Yours in success,

Regan x

DID YOU LOVE THIS BOOK?

*I*f you did, it would mean the world to me if you could take two minutes and head on over to the store you bought this book from and leave a review on this book! I'd be forever grateful and would LOVE to hear from you and about your experience!

Even if you purchased this book through my website or were gifted it (you must have cool friends giving you a gift like this!), you can still head over to Amazon and search for either the book name or my name, click "Leave A Review" and let us know what you thought!

Thank you so much!

And remember, you absolutely can have it all!

Regan x

HOW CAN REGAN HELP YOU FURTHER?

$\mathcal{A}$re you committed to achieving success without limits? Trust me when I say, you absolutely CAN have it all, HOWEVER, you NEED to do the WORK!

If you have enjoyed this book and are ready to do the inner work required to accelerate your success, then I know you're going to love working with me.

As mentioned above, I work with people on a range of different levels, from online masterminds, to live masterminds, to bigger live events, right through to high-end one-to-one coaching.

However, where everyone starts, is to join Your SuccessHub, become a part of the tribe and access the weekly success coaching to take your life and your business to the next level.

Follow the link to lock in an amazing 50% off the normal Your SuccessHub monthly access fee! For you, the coaching is just $97 USD a month instead of the usual $197 USD a month! And, that is for as long as you choose to stay — no price increase for you, ever! You can cancel at any time, too.

http://reganhillyer.com/successhub/

As a tribe member accessing Your SuccessHub weekly coaching, you will receive:

- Weekly online success coaching from Regan
- PDFs and worksheets to accelerate your learning
- Access to the online support and coaching group: "The Success Tribe" so you can ask Regan any questions about the trainings

- The ability to request personal coaching topics
- Networking opportunities with an incredible community of amazing people committed to their success!

Examples of the types of things covered in the training:

- Removing unconscious blocks limiting you
- How to set up your day for success
- The fast tracks to having it all in your life
- Dealing with fear and overcoming limits
- Removing self-sabotaging behaviour once and for all
- The secret of the 2%
- Learn how to compound your success
- Untapped life and business hacks
- And much, MUCH more! (Remember there is a new coaching topic every week!)

If you have enjoyed what you have learned in this book and are ready to join the tribe, then we welcome you with open arms!

What are you waiting for?

Head on over and join the tribe as the 50% off offer will not be alive forever!

http://reganhillyer.com/successhub/

ABOUT THE AUTHOR

*H*i! I'm Regan Hillyer
My mission is to unlock your greatness, disrupt your version of "normal" and let you know that you can become wildly successful, now. A world traveler at heart, I pride myself on making a massive impact in this world and showing people that they can be extraordinary, because there's lots of room at the top!

I am a best selling author, an international speaker, entrepreneur and coach. I have founded The Be Your Brand Mastermind LIVE, The Online Empire Builder, Your SuccessHub Weekly Success Coaching, amongst other incredible live events and online programs. Everything I do gives back and supports the Lumière Project, with the mission to help people ignite their flames and unleash their true message on the world.

I am an expert when it comes to working with people one-to-one and in small mastermind groups and, I would love to help you create a business and a life that you love, allowing you to have it all in every area of your life, on your terms!

A Kiwi girl who tried to do it all right — go to school, get good grades, go to university… And one day I figured out that there was definitely more to life. With a ridiculous work ethic, a heart of service and a laptop, I've created my socially-conscious empire from scratch. With a global approach to success and development, I'm here to tell you that you really CAN have it all…

I don't do labels, but if I had to have one, it would be a "serial-entrepreneur" because like you, there are many things that I love taking to the next level.

I believe that you need to bring your complete game to the the business table and, if you want to stand out and be successful in today's world, then that includes your personality, your vibe, your tribe and most importantly your hunger to succeed. I'm known to deliver high quality, out of the box, say it like it is, break the rules, business and personal development training.

Your success is what drives me to help you get better and better results! I'm always creating, and I'd love for you to join my newsletter to get first access. You can subscribe over at www.reganhillyer.com

My commitment to you is 100%. To always bring you the very best of what I have and what I'm learning and to keep it real and raw as I go.

Make sure you subscribe to www.reganhillyer.com

You can learn more about me here: http://www.reganhillyer.com/about-regan/

And make sure you connect on Facebook over here: https://www.facebook.com/ReganHillyer

Check out Your SuccessHub weekly success coaching and find out how I can help you do the inner work required to take your life and your business to the next level at http://reganhillyer.com/successhub/

See you at the top!

And remember, you absolutely can have it all!

Regan x